Alternative Careers for TEACHERS

MARNA L. BEARD
and MICHAEL J. McGAHEY

ARCO PUBLISHING, INC.
NEW YORK

To JAMES L. DOOLEY, Mentor

Second Edition, First Printing

Published by Arco Publishing, Inc.
215 Park Avenue South, New York, N.Y. 10003

Copyright © 1985, 1983 by Marna L. Beard and Michael J. McGahey

All rights reserved. No part of this book may
be reproduced, by any means, without permission
in writing from the publisher, except by a
reviewer who wishes to quote brief excerpts in
connection with a review in a magazine or
newspaper.

Library of Congress Cataloging in Publication Data

Beard, Marna L.
  Alternative careers for teachers.

  Bibliography: p.
  Includes index.
  1. Career changes. 2. Job hunting. 3. Vocational
guidance. 4. Teaching—Vocational guidance. I. McGahey,
Michael J. II. Title.
HF5384.B4   1985   650.1'4'024372   84-24460
ISBN 0-668-06373-4 (pbk.)

Printed in the United States of America

CONTENTS

    ACKNOWLEDGMENTS   v
    PREFACE   vi
1. THERE IS LIFE AFTER TEACHING   1
2. THE EXPERIENCE OF OTHERS   13
3. PLANNING MAKES IT HAPPEN BETTER   29
4. FINDING YOUR WAY   39
5. WITH YOUR CERTIFICATION, CONSIDER . . .   58
6. OCCUPATIONAL RESEARCH   137
7. RESUMES   150
8. MARKETING STRATEGIES   171
9. SETTING THE STAGE FOR CHANGE   182

    APPENDIX I. JOBS IN THE FEDERAL GOVERNMENT BY COLLEGE MAJOR   199
    APPENDIX II. MATCHING PERSONAL AND JOB CHARACTERISTICS   219
    APPENDIX III. GUIDE TO FEDERAL CAREER LITERATURE   230
    BIBLIOGRAPHY   245
    AUTHORS' NOTE   249
    INDEX   250

ACKNOWLEDGMENTS

No work of this nature is ever created without the assistance and input of many individuals. The authors gratefully acknowledge:

The many teachers and former teachers who shared so willingly their experiences and insights;

Joan Stark, Dean of the College of Education at The University of Michigan, for providing and permitting use of the findings of research into the various careers of accredited teachers;

The United States Department of Labor for their analysis, organization, and publication of a wealth of occupational information;

Margaret McGahey and Paul DeGrieck for their suggestions and journalistic expertise;

Vicki Adams for her skill in deciphering and typing;

The friends, colleagues, and family members who offered valuable support.

PREFACE

Meeting forks in the road, finding choices before us that may ultimately influence the whole of our later lives, gives us reason to pause and assess the situation. You no doubt picked up this book because you are at a fork in the road.

Teachers, confined as they are to school settings, often know little about the world of business and industry. A first reaction when facing a career change is to back up—to return to school and retrain. Yet, educators do have interesting and rewarding career avenues that are accessible directly from teaching. If you have been successful thus far in life, there is no reason to doubt your ability to be successful in a new career.

Toward your continued success we offer this book of personal awareness, of career information, of the experience of other teachers, of encouragement, of directions to take and suggestions to try. Above all, we offer affirmation that you have the power to travel the road of your choice, and that such personal power is both invigorating and sufficient to overcome almost any obstacle in your path.

Godspeed.

M.L.B.
M.J.M.

1.

THERE IS LIFE AFTER TEACHING

*What else can I do?
I'm just a teacher!*

A competent teacher performs many complex tasks. The experience of teaching develops and refines desirable skills. Consequently, if you are a teacher considering alternative careers, recognize that you are not "just a teacher." You are a highly educated and skilled person who has chosen teaching and who can also choose to use your many competencies in other endeavors. Your broad range of abilities, your education and experience give you flexibility. It is a myth that teachers have few marketable talents; many alternatives to teaching do exist. You will start seeing options for yourself as you recognize the usefulness and value of your many skills.

Start by considering your education. Less than 15 percent of the workforce in the United States has attained a college degree. As a teacher you are in the top 15 percent of the populace educationally. Teachers are outstanding learners. You must learn something before you can teach it, and you do this regularly. Learning ability alone is an asset in any career. But your demonstrated ability as a capable learner is only part of the good news.

The *Dictionary of Occupational Titles (D.O.T.)* is a reference book available in almost any library. This U.S. Government publication defines and classifies over 20,000 occupations found in the United States. A number is assigned to each occupation. Part of the *D.O.T.* number rates each occupation by the complexity involved in dealing with data, people, and things. The data, people, and things code for teaching is 228. This means that teachers deal with data at an analytic and problem-solving level and with people at an instructional level, one step beyond the supervision level. (The 8 indicates no significant involvement with things.) So teachers deal with data and people at sophisticated levels, and this ability has application outside the classroom. A look at the *Dictionary of Occupational Titles* will show you how very capable teachers are, based on job function ratings that analyze the world of work. But you don't have to look that far to discover the talents and skills teachers possess.

We sat down with a group of teachers and did a fifteen-minute brainstorming exercise to identify some of the tasks and responsibilities that are a regular part of teaching. The following list evolved, and it is by no means all-inclusive:

    organization of environment
    organization of time and materials
    management of students
    problem solving
    conflict resolution
    testing
    recordkeeping
    public relations work
    mediation
    material design and production
    evaluation of materials
    evaluation of student aptitudes
    evaluation of student performances
    public speaking
    motivation and persuasion
    instruction (conveying ideas clearly)
    needs assessment, analysis and teaching by objective
    self-evaluation
    using technical equipment (computers, media equipment, office equipment)
    research
    task analysis

THERE IS LIFE AFTER TEACHING

writing
planning
learning
consulting
using group dynamics insights and skills
adapting to new situations
designing new projects
supervising
crowd control (Someone was thinking of lunch duty!)

As a teacher you might take performance of these activities for granted, but the world at large is deficient in the skills which you have developed and now possess. For example, the TV show *Real People* recently broadcast the results of a survey done to determine what people most feared. To their surprise, they found people did not fear spiders, snakes, or natural disasters as much as they feared having to speak in front of a group. At this time raise your right hand, reach over your shoulder and pat yourself on the back. You have mastered, as a teacher, one of the world's most frightening situations—speaking to groups.

Teachers need to look at their lives and work experiences in new ways and to get away from a narrow perception of their skills.

Joan S. Stark, Dean of the School of Education at the University of Michigan, recently reported the results of a follow-up study on persons who had received teaching certificates from that university between 1946 and 1976. One goal of this research was to assess the career opportunities of the 673 career teachers sampled and to compare them with the opportunities of the 646 noneducators (certified teachers working outside of education). She and her associates found that "even in a tight job market, those who prepared for teaching are finding ways to use their skills well, often in jobs with brighter advancement prospects and higher salaries than teaching."[1]

---

[1] Joan S. Stark, Ann E. Austin, Malcolm A. Lowther, David W. Chapman, Sigrid M. Hutcheson, "Teacher Certification Recipients at the University of Michigan 1946 through 1976: A 1980 Follow-up Study, " *Innovator*, Vol. 12, No. 8 (March 30, 1981), p. 2.

ALTERNATIVE CAREERS FOR TEACHERS

Teacher preparation was found to be a ticket to a wide variety of positions. This research found the 646 noneducators working in seventy different careers. Table 1 lists the most frequent occupations cited.

TABLE 1[2]

Most Frequent Occupations of Noneducators with Teacher Certification

(These University of Michigan graduates awarded teaching certificates, taught briefly or not at all.)

Position	Frequency	Percent
business administrator	61	9.4
lawyer/judge	38	5.9
secretary	33	5.1
librarian/historian/museum curator	31	4.8
sales representative	31	4.8
computer programmer/scientist/engineering analyst	21	3.3
business owner	20	3.1
government administrator	19	2.9
real estate agent	18	2.8
hospital administrator	17	2.6
accountant/treasurer	14	2.2
editor/publisher	14	2.2
nonteaching psychologist	14	2.2
insurance agent	14	2.2
educational consultant	13	2.0
social worker	13	2.0
legal aide/legal stenographer	11	1.7
music director/musician	11	1.7
social welfare/recreational supervisor	11	1.7
bookkeeper	11	1.7
clergy	11	1.7
(49) other job titles	220	34.0
	646	100.0

---

[2]Stark and others, "Teacher Certification," p. 21.

THERE IS LIFE AFTER TEACHING

SKILLS DO TRANSFER

Teaching involves many talents and skills that have application outside the field of education. Teachers generally exhibit high levels of verbal and analytic thinking skills. They are also conscientious, dependable, imaginative, perceptive, independent, responsible, and mature. Teachers have strong interpersonal relation skills; they can motivate, counsel, coordinate, discipline, manage, and consult. These skills will aid you in almost any new career you choose.

Even skills that you might at first think unique to teaching have application outside the classroom. We learned of one ex-teacher who went to work in a Hallmark Card shop. After a month on the job, she was asked to redo the window display. She is now a regional window designer for Hallmark. Even all that bulletin board practice can be useful outside the classroom!

Don't forget the skills and knowledge you have acquired through volunteer work, hobbies, and leisure activities. A former electronics teacher is now an art dealer with his own studio. He regularly travels to Europe to purchase art. A former art teacher now runs his own lawn care and landscape business. A former English teacher is a teaching pro at a tennis club. A former social studies teacher is entering commercial photography, and a former music teacher is enjoying greater harmony as an auto mechanic. All told, you probably have a greater variety of abilities than you realize.

Have you ever moved your household from one home to another? If so, you undoubtedly were surprised at discovering how many belongings you had collected through the years. Career development is like that—you acquire a variety of competencies, interests, and experiences in the process of working, living, and learning. As you now consider a career move, and pause to sort through what you have accumulated, you will likely be surprised at all the assets you have acquired. Since career development is a growth process, nothing in your current career is wasted. You have been enriched by your experiences. You

ALTERNATIVE CAREERS FOR TEACHERS

can now move much of your accumulated career wealth and still make great use of it; skills and abilities are transferable.

A former teacher, currently a personnel manager, has seen how her teaching skills transfer to her new career:

>Teaching helped me to become a fairly good judge of character. I now evaluate resumes but also look at grooming, speech, personality, the bright eyes—lots of those cues that teachers learn to recognize and use on a daily basis. I think the skills most transferable were the management or leadership skills. I was in charge for a long time as a teacher, responsible for the planning, the personnel, and the objectives. Management by objective is not new to teachers; they do it hour by hour.

A self-employed businessman states:

>Teachers are almost naturals for marketing and sales careers. They are experienced at anticipating needs, giving presentations, listening and responding, motivating and evaluating. Sales is very closely related to teaching.

A placement counselor at an employment agency told us:

>Teachers have exhibited all the qualities necessary for managing. They are strong on organizational and personal relations skills. We have encountered a high interest in employing teachers for management positions in the restaurant and fast food industry. The work involves dealing with young, unskilled workers, and teachers can handle the toughest parts of the job—instructing, supervising, managing, and motivating.

Communication skills are also transferable. Surprisingly, a lot of people in the workforce don't have strong communication skills. You would be amazed at the number of people who are highly skilled in technical areas but who cannot express their knowledge in written form. Technical writing, customer education, and the writing of training programs are all areas where skills that teachers possess have application. Couple these

THERE IS LIFE AFTER TEACHING

communication skills with a teacher's analytic ability and understanding of people, and a broad range of options emerge.

A former teacher shared this:

> Teaching skills do transfer. Teachers are not afraid to ask questions, to accept responsibility, to learn even from mistakes. Have you ever noticed those ads that say, "Must Be a Self-Starter"? Well, teachers sure are—they do it all! It's this kind of maturity that I see evident in ex-teachers in new careers.
>
> Teachers are also very ingenious at coming up with ways to explain things. You have to be when you instruct kids who have only limited life experiences and you must explain things to them. This ingenuity is a skill I find useful even in my computer programming career. I'm still developing new ways to communicate and to create understanding—only now I'm helping computers and people to make sense of each other.

The most interesting thing about all these skills is that they have been advanced and refined to become personal attributes. They are not skills that any employer or quick course can readily teach, *but you have them!* Think back to your first days in teaching. Do you remember that initial year—the strain of anticipating student needs, planning, organizing, evaluating, and all the mental fatigue that resulted? You were growing through that experience and have been since. In the process of becoming a teacher, by helping others to learn and to achieve, you also learned and achieved. Most teachers admit that they didn't learn to teach in the College of Education. We learned to teach by teaching. These skills add up to leadership, the ability to organize and to direct. This demonstrated leadership ability, and the self-assurance which goes with it, is useful everywhere. Leadership is the reason successful teachers have become successful in many other careers.

It is time to forget your dependence on the college credentials and state certification codes that were so all-important when you entered your teaching career. Those credentials do not do justice to the proficiencies you now possess. You do not need legal certifications to do most other work; you need only to be able to demonstrate that you can do the job, or learn to do it. Take stock of your many skills, market them, and gain the additional training you may desire within your next career. Liberal arts graduates have always followed that course. So can you!

When others suggest that you retrain, they offer a simplistic answer to your complex career dilemma. If you accept retraining as a course of action, you may just be postponing solving your career problem. Retraining can be costly, in both time and money. Wait to decide about retraining until you are already engaged in a new career. You can then identify what specific training, if any, will be of practical benefit. Your employer may even subsidize that additional education.

REWARDS OF CHANGING CAREERS

By doing some self-analysis and career research, you become more aware of your valuable skills and their range of application. You also prepare yourself for any adjustments you may face in moving out of education. The unknown can be intimidating merely because it is unknown. The University of Michigan study found job satisfaction among those certified teachers employed outside of education to be equivalent to that of career teachers.[3] While there are adjustments in making a career change, they can be pleasant. For some, the career change involves giving up something that is good for something potentially better. For others, the change from teaching brings a welcome new way of life.

These statements from three former teachers illustrate some of the changes:

---
[3]Stark and others, "Teacher Certification," p. 29.

THERE IS LIFE AFTER TEACHING

There were adjustments in moving out of education, but I liked most of them. There's much more socializing with adults in the business world and I have enjoyed this aspect of my career change immensely. I find it interesting and stimulating being exposed to minds as good or better than mine.

I also like the autonomy. I'm free from that class schedule and bells ringing every forty-five minutes. I find I'm competing more with myself, challenging myself, identifying objectives and mapping out the way there. The whole business world is more competitive; everyone strives to prove that they are contributing. But, there is recognition, too. If you introduce a new program here, it is immediately apparent; whereas in a school, your new teaching approach or unit could go unnoticed for years. I enjoy the autonomy, this competition, and the opportunities for recognition and advancement.

Other advantages are that my work surroundings are pleasant, there is no aggression to deal with, and my personal safety is assured. When you ask me what I miss, I'd say the kids—some of them, that is. And, that I am no longer "Number 1" on stage like I had been in the classroom. As a teacher I was something of a ham at heart. I had fun with that captive audience!

* * * * * * * * *

Offer me $50,000 to teach and I'd say, "Keep it!" The life outside is one devil of a lot better. It's the best thing I ever did. When I think back on that other life—what a contrast! There is no more raising my voice or being upset. What a relief to be away from the horsing around, the constant complaining and irresponsibility: "I forgot it . . . . That's not fair . . . . Can I go get it now? . . . . I lost it . . . . Gee, I didn't think of that . . . . How come we have to . . . . ?"

I am a new person. In twenty years I've never had the health that I have now. I enjoy meeting lots of interesting people, really nice people. I'm enjoying my new career freedom. Once you get out you get so many more career opportunities. My resume now looks great. I've done so many things in the last four years—wow, has it been that long already! Oh, I could go on and on about the differences. For me the change has brought so many pluses, it's, well, just *happiness!*

* * * * * * * * *

When I was teaching, there was no end to my work. As much as you do as a teacher, there is always more that needs to be done. Now that stress, that tension is gone. There is an end to my day's work. Weekends and evenings are my own and I can relax and enjoy them and my family without feeling uneasy about some set of papers that needs checking. I sleep better and truly feel like a totally different person, one who is enjoying all of life more.

When you ask me about losses, I'm tempted to say I've lost having summers off, but with my weekends and evenings really mine, my vacation time has just been cut down and spread out. So many teachers talk about hanging in, just making it until June, that for them summers are like R and R—the rest and recuperation given to soldiers. They seem to live through nine months waiting for three. No, I really don't think I've lost anything. And I know I've gained much. My future looks super! I've had the opportunity to learn new things and have taken about ten in-house courses during work hours in the past two years. That training, this great work experience, and the undersupply in this field mean that I have a future with many more opportunities.

MAKING IT HAPPEN

Imagination is a necessary ingredient in the art of living. Imagining that you can do other things, believing in yourself, is the first step in creating a career change. If you see yourself exclusively as a teacher, unlikely to be able to do anything else, then you will remain exclusively a teacher. You won't be able to do anything else. All of the world's important discoveries began with someone's imagination. If you wish to discover a new career direction, you must first imagine some possibilities.

Fear, another kind of imagining, can get in your way and keep you stuck. A person learning to swim might have all the skills—the stroke, the breathing, the kick—but not be able to swim because he fears taking his feet off the bottom. He imagines sinking. You have many skills and the ability to change careers, but if you can't visualize yourself doing it, if you have a fear of sinking, then you won't move either. Your energy will be spent instead in resistance—worry, depression, procrastination, anger, indecision, disorganization—all fear-induced, self-defeating behaviors.

If your goal is to create a career change, start to imagine it and believe it. Visualize it. Be open to acquiring new insights into both yourself and the world of work. A sense of direction will evolve from the exploring you do and the knowledge that you accumulate. Stepping stones will appear almost naturally. Imagination will lead to curiosity, curiosity to discovery, discovery to goal setting, goal setting to action, and action ultimately to a new career.

Positive thinking can also help you over many hurdles along the way. Consider the words of Winston Churchill: "I am an optimist. It does not seem much use being anything else."

Teachers have many skills and competencies. Although there is a demand for these talents, no ready market exists for all teachers seeking career change. Initiative and active searching are required. While adjustments are associated with change, ex-teachers have found that many skills used and developed in teaching have transferred to serve in new careers. They have also discovered satisfactions, opportunities, and benefits derived from careers outside education. The process of career change is an easier one if met with enthusiasm and optimism. One must imagine that a career change is possible before it can occur. Then in making the change actually happen, commitment to action is the key.

A former teacher, now a public relations specialist, shares these thoughts on commitment:

ALTERNATIVE CAREERS FOR TEACHERS

I finally made up my mind that I wasn't going to leave this city until I found something for myself outside of education. I told my wife and kids to go up to the cottage or do whatever, but that I was determined to make a career change happen now. It took me two phone calls and a meeting with each of those two contacts to get a start in my current career.

A teacher wanting a change must eventually be psychologically ready to take action to find something else. You can read, sit, think, and analyze forever. Too much of that just amounts to analysis paralysis and leads nowhere. Go and <u>do</u> something! Love yourself enough to be good to yourself and to those around you. Act. Call some people. Put feelers out and get moving. Just make up your mind and do it!

Living involves choosing. Your way of life is the product of your choosing. Power resides in you. You always have that power of choice in your hands, power that controls your thoughts and imaginings, your feelings, your attitudes, and your actions. You can choose to think and act creatively in self-enhancing ways to improve your life or work setting. You can transplant yourself and continue growing in a new environment, if you so choose.

As a teacher you have many career options because of your demonstrated proficiencies. You are "just a teacher" only if you see yourself that narrowly. In truth, teachers are multi-talented learners and achievers, very responsible individuals. Consequently, they are also highly successful in many other careers.

2.

THE EXPERIENCE OF OTHERS

Anxious moments do accompany a career change. All change has some stress associated with it. Our initial research for this book showed that teachers contemplating a career change felt more confident if they knew colleagues who had already made successful transitions. This reinforces the truth that we can benefit from the experience of others.

To offer some reassurance and to provide you with better understanding of the career change experience, we introduce fifteen teachers who have already made the transition from education. Their varied comments provide valuable insights and many words of encouragement. As you explore the many employment possibilities outside of education, you are likely to meet other successful former teachers. You will probably find yourself experiencing less anxiety, and, like people we've met, feeling excited about your own career future.

Register Representative

As a register representative I sell securities, insurance, annuities, I.R.A.'s. The company I work for has an excellent training program and has hired lots of ex-teachers who have done quite well in this field. Ex-teachers are particularly skilled in their ability to make presentations to clients, to match the presentation to the client's level of education, to read the client throughout the presentation, and to alter the presentation if necessary. The teachers are also analytic and self-directed, both valuable qualities.

In fact, teachers who are self-directed are overwhelmed with excitement at the possibilities out here. They are amazed at the potential! A friend of mine, a former teacher, just called me from the South where he is in training with a major corporation. He was delighted to find out that his company ties a bonus to the scores received on tests during this training period. After four weeks he has had 100 percent on every test; he's elated.

I have known lots of teachers seeking career transitions; however, not all of them have had positive experiences. I'm immediately reminded of a group of five teachers who got together for support in their career change and turned their meetings into complaint sessions. All five are still drawing unemployment.

Previous to becoming a register representative, I spent eleven years in education. Nine of those years were in the classroom, teaching junior high math and special education. My last two years were spent in administration of special education programs at a county level. I personally subscribe to the philosophy that I would rather try something and fail than wish at a later age that I had tried it. This philosophy influenced my change.

Health Education Technician

I have a BA degree with a major in sociology and a minor in political science. I taught language arts on the middle school level. I also taught childbirth classes to adults. Today I am employed in the continuing education department of a large metropolitan hospital as a health education technician. I plan and develop health education programs. Right now I am involved in planning a child passenger project which deals with car seats, seat belts, etc. I represent the hospital on a metropolitan task force, give presentations to schools where we sometimes pre- and post-test for the effectiveness of the educational program, and speak to community groups. A new exciting

THE EXPERIENCE OF OTHERS

project is working on the closed circuit TV programming in the hospital and writing scripts.

My teaching skills of planning, developing ideas and projects, dealing with the community, public speaking, and working with children are used in this position.

I obtained this job through personal contacts, networking. My advice to you is, Don't be afraid to use your contacts! I was at first, but I've gotten over that. If I think I can do a job, I press into service any contacts I have.

Training Specialist

Changing careers is the best move I ever made for myself. I had taught business education classes in the same high school for six and a half years. Like many colleagues, I chose to sponsor extracurricular activities, work on a district curriculum committee, and plan courses within my department. I enjoyed teaching but the experience of being pink-slipped, called back, pink-slipped, called back certainly affected the amount of enthusiasm I was able to generate and sustain for the position.

As I began to examine options I found I knew very little about the world of business and industry. I did a great deal of reading and learning about job search methods. It paid off. The job I accepted was to develop employee training programs for a large bank in a metropolitan area. In this position as a training specialist, I am responsible for designing, developing, implementing, and conducting staff training workshops for the clerical and secretarial employees. A recent promotion, after only one and a half years, will provide me the challenge of developing similar programs for credit analysts.

I really like my new career. There are lots of challenging opportunities in the position. I feel quite comfortable in the job because I use all of the skills used in teaching. Most helpful to me is my knowledge of publishing companies and their materials, audio-visual equipment, teaching techniques, and curriculum development. My experience in speaking to groups is a real plus.

Several teaching colleagues of mine also changed careers. We helped each other through the process. I enjoyed listening and sharing ideas with them. I think you'll find others willing to help you.

Sales Representative

My present career as a sales representative has evolved from many previous positions. It's interesting to view it from this perspective. I taught high school social studies for four years before I began a master's program. After I obtained my MA degree, I taught in a college setting, training teachers for a federally funded project. There were no teaching materials available for this project, so I began writing some and found a publisher interested in printing them. It didn't take me long to figure out that the sales people were making a whole lot more off my materials than I was drawing in royalty checks. I then became self-employed and worked on commission as a sales representative for five companies whose product lines were educational materials.

I now represent only one company and have a salary plus commission. I choose products for the company, do workshops, and make sales presentations. I find my present job very rewarding. I still draw on many of my teaching skills—my ability to advance ideas and to work with a variety of people on any educational level. You have those skills too, regardless of the level you teach, because you find the same spectrum of educational backgrounds in the parents you communicate with daily.

I am treated very professionally in the business world, not at all like a second-class citizen. I have made many friends nationwide and met many former teachers. My company recently hired several new sales representatives; the requirements were a master's degree and classroom teaching experience.

THE EXPERIENCE OF OTHERS

My only suggestion to you is to attend carefully to your resume. There is a joke in the business world about receiving resumes from teachers with misspelled words. A hospital administrator, incidentally a former teacher, related how he scanned 200 resumes for an administrative position in ten minutes. His secretary had previously screened them to determine if they possessed the necessary qualifications. In those ten minutes he only looked at the layout of the resume and was able to narrow the field of applicants to a manageable size. Take great care in the preparation of your resume.

Outreach Coordinator for a Historical Society

I left teaching and ended up creating my own teaching career. I'll explain.

I had taught English and French for six and a half years at the junior high level. Then I had children and took a leave of absence. While I was on leave, the school system dropped foreign languages. Being dissatisfied with the balance of teaching opportunities, I took an extended leave. I first went to work for the Social Security Administration, thinking that there I'd find security (no pun intended). I ended up very unhappy with that job, the lack of training offered, the bureaucracy, and the paper shuffling. I finally resigned.

A local historical site was advertising for guides. I applied. They were just beginning their program of doing living history. The education and history curators generated guidelines and then enlisted employees to create interpretive history programs. I had done some theater work in high school and college, and was a speech major along with my background in English and French. I teamed with another employee to recreate the French and Indian life of our area with costumes, props, everything. The concept and program were a success and I loved the job.

Since the site closed for the winter, I decided to search actively for another position that would allow me to continue doing the same things. My partner and I developed an historical presentation, wrote a brochure, and marketed our show to schools within the immediate area. The historical site provided us costumes and props. The positive response was enough to support financially only one member of our team of two. We approached the local historical society and became contract employees and then applied for and received a grant. Our programs are booked full time and continue annually to attract greater interest.

All of my teaching skills are still in use. In addition to writing, developing, and presenting new "living history" programs, I have done public relations work, marketing, video taping, and am now a trainer of volunteer costumed interpreters. I've developed teaching packets, assembled slide shows, and designed follow-up activities all related to our programs. I'm teaching like never before. If funding should be withdrawn, "Plan B" is to go independent in contracting our performances. At this point, I believe we could succeed.

When you consider career change, realize that you are the only one who knows you. Sit down and list everything that you know how to do. Break down your teaching job to its most minute particles and also consider volunteer work, college experiences, everything! Then decide what you really want to do, what you would be happiest doing.

Security was an issue when I first left teaching; I'm oriented that way. Teachers tend to emphasize security. I had to rethink that a whole lot. Rather than looking for security first, think about what you really want to do. When you get into doing things you want, you will see avenues to do other things you can do, and so on. What a terrible sacrifice in personal happiness you can pay for security!

Free-Lance Writer and Educational Consultant

Teachers wishing to change careers should keep in mind that there are several routes to take: (1) back to school for reeducation in another field, (2) straight into the job market with hope for advancement, and (3) an often neglected route, volunteerism. While everyone cannot opt for volunteerism, it opened many doors for me.

After seventeen years in education, having been an English teacher, sex education teacher, counselor, and principal, I quit teaching. I worked for two years as a volunteer counselor at a federal prison. This gave me useful insights and experience which led to a full-time position in a juvenile justice agency. Frankly, that position wasn't very different from teaching.

Personal associates informed me that a national magazine was looking for a person to work on an educational award project. They needed an individual who had both a writing and teaching background. I interviewed and was assigned the project. That opportunity gave me an "in" and I later convinced them to let me write a monthly column. I parlayed those two writing experiences into getting articles published in other magazines, at first on education, later on related subjects. During the past four years I have written mostly books.

The writing experiences have led naturally to speaking engagements. The speaking exposures have led to educational consulting experiences for a variety of organizations, even a game company. My schedule is full and I don't have a full-time position with any one company.

Teaching seems to me to be the fullest background you can have to prepare you for any other job, because you teach people, not subjects. You teach them intimately enough to get inside them, to know them. Your understanding of young people and their parents—their needs, fears, hurts, and problems—as well as your recognition of the power of a good self-image, your ability to speak in front of people, and your ability to handle the English language, will naturally transfer with you in new options.

Educational Representative for a Newspaper

The teachers I know who are now in the business world are very happy. Compared to every day with kids and all the papers, other jobs seem far less tiring. It's really nice to be able to make your own schedule. Every day is different.

I work in the educational department of a large newspaper. Four out of five days I spend some part of the day in a school setting. I do workshops for educators on the use of the newspaper, make presentations at conventions and educational conferences, and prepare materials for the teachers to use.

As one might expect, I obtained my job by answering a newspaper ad. One hundred fifty people responded to the ad, which requested that the applicant have a teaching background, preferably with some sales experience. My teaching background came from three years in elementary education. I had some sales experience from an interim position where I sold special education materials.

I really like my position; it's the best of two worlds. I like the contacts with teachers. I appreciate learning from them, hearing what is happening in the classroom, and sharing new ideas with them. And I like my freedom.

Stockbroker

I would advise teachers wanting a career change to "go for it." Jobs won't come looking for you; you'll have to go looking for them. See people personally—don't merely write letters or send resumes.

I had taught for five years at the elementary level and for ten years at the university level in social studies. I obtained my current position by answering a blind ad in the newspaper.

As a stockbroker I sell stocks, corporate bonds, options, municipal bonds, annuities, unit trusts, mutual funds, life insurance, federal securities, limited partnerships, and financial futures.

Skills and abilities that transferred from teaching include: working with people, clear goal setting, organizing ability, hard work, administrative ability, computer experience, working under pressure and within deadlines, and working occasionally with irate people.

I know many—I'd say over a hundred—former teachers who have moved from education to other successful careers. Go for it!

Personnel, Coordinator QWL Program

I enjoyed my years in education but wanted a change, an opportunity to see what options existed for me in business. I have an MA in guidance and counseling. My undergraduate work was in business administration and psychology.

I knew I wanted a job in personnel. My skills would be transferable; the audience would just be different. Pride interfered with my making initial contacts to start networking, but I soon overcame that. The first really desirable position I interviewed for was in career counseling at a large metropolitan hospital. I had to convince them that a health care background was not necessary, that in fact, the field of education is the leader in career development. They believed; I had my first position.

It took a short time before I was really comfortable in that position, because the language, the jargon, was different. I had many assignments related to the continuing education of hospital personnel and also conducted new employee orientations. The opportunity came to move into management development where I set up workshops and did consulting, counseling, and lots of listening. This was a lateral move which I took to gain experience. I always try to use a position to build on my skills.

My career has taken another twist. Following a workshop presentation, I was approached with an offer of a new career opportunity. I am now involved in coordinating a QWL (quality of work life) program for a group of hospitals in three states. Our goal is to enhance the work environment for employees. We use a variety of assessment tools to develop problem-solving methods based on the collected data. This was a totally new position for me even though I had done some of these things on a considerably smaller scale. Needless to say, this is an extremely exciting position with the potential to lead to even more responsible and challenging opportunities. It is quite a jump from that first career counseling job, and a jump made in relatively few years.

How did I get where I am today? Well, I'd like to think one factor was that I do a good job, am innovative, and am an able learner. However, that certainly isn't all of it. Other factors were influential, too. I was willing to take a salary cut, or move laterally, to gain experience. The decrease I took to get first-line supervision experience was very helpful in advancing my career. Mentors have helped me temendously. I owe them a lot. I have found mentors in every place I've worked. One other thing I think was an asset is my belief in developing professional visibility—both internally and externally—in any position. These things have been helpful to me; in all likelihood, they could be factors helpful to you.

Assistant Manager, Bank Branch Operations

The desire to work with people was what led me into the banking industry after being laid off from teaching. Many bankers, like teachers, are people people. Extremely complex relationships develop when people confide their intimate financial and personal lives.

I had worked in banking as a teller during summers while I attended college, and returned to banking after one year of teaching high school business subjects. Skills in organization and evaluation are perhaps the most obvious ones that transferred from teaching to my current career.

As the branch operations assistant manager I am responsible for coordinating the teller area and general operations of the branch. This includes staffing, scheduling, reconciling differences, writing monthly reports, teller evaluation and raises, public and customer relations, service for all accounts, and counseling in the areas of new accounts, loans, mortgages, and bonds.

Regarding career change, confidence without cockiness is important. Any job can be learned. Training programs, such as the one provided for me, exist in many facets of business. As educators and former students we have proven already that we can learn.

Marketing Research Manager

I recall that things looked awfully bleak when I left teaching. My teaching experience consisted only of two semesters of student teaching—junior high English in an urban setting. The experience dispelled any illusions I had about teaching. I realized I could not be the kind of educator I had dreamed of being, so I chose to find something else. I could not have picked a more difficult time for myself to change careers since I got married as soon as I graduated. My wife and I discussed matters, and then we both worked part time while I returned to school to complete a major in journalism.

With that out of the way, I went to work as a reporter. During the next year I worked for two different newspapers. The pay was no better than that of a teacher and the hours were much worse! Having spent an extra year preparing for a journalism career and after a year as a reporter, I found that I didn't enjoy that career either. I was 0 for 2 and things really looked bleak!

A referral from the head of the journalism department at the university led to an interview with a major manufacturing firm and to a start in a very satisfying advertising/marketing career. I was hired because I could write—something the corporation could not teach. I was then provided a ten-week study course on advertising. I learned through practical experience from there, becoming responsible for the advertising budget of two divisions within the corporation.

I utilized that experience in moving to a smaller firm where I have assumed more responsibilities. As a marketing research manager I assemble and analyze information about the markets in which my company operates. I gather data from industry sources, from associations, from research firms, and through original research, and use that information to develop marketing recommendations. These reports to the executive committee identify areas of the country either where new markets are developing or where our share of industry sales could be improved.

I do liaison work with an advertising agency for national consumer and trade advertising and am responsible for a 1.3-million-dollar budget. I analyze the effectiveness of advertising through surveys, through data gathered by dealers, and through receipt of coupons clipped from ads. While the agency writes the actual ads and recommends which media to use, we can approve or veto their suggestions.

I write, organize, and follow through on dealer advertising—brochures, displays, posters, salesmen's aids, and other material typically found in a dealership.

Essentially, the skills I use are planning and organizing, writing clearly and concisely, and presenting ideas convincingly. I used these same skills in teaching.

Some teachers who change careers may, like me, find that the second career is no more satisfying than the first. Does that mean you go back to teaching as the lesser of two evils? Not necessarily. Go on to that third career. Keep trying, buoyed by belief in your own ability, until you find the job that's right for you. And make no mistake about it, you will find one.

Owner and Vice-President of Supply Business

I have learned so much away from teaching and have so much more to learn that I look forward to the future with the greatest excitement. I am actually disappointed when Friday arrives because there are so many things that I was not able to accomplish.

THE EXPERIENCE OF OTHERS

I am involved in every aspect of the school supply business which my husband and I started. I do workshops in the schools, demonstrate computer software, visit school principals and curriculum people, bid on consumable supplies, order materials, and fend off our C.P.A. (because of our heavy inventory). Teachers enjoy learning new things, and in this business there is something new every day.

One of the adjustments you face in moving into business and sales is that you are no longer one hundred percent manager. Clients and customers are more in charge; there is an external type of evaluation. The results of your work can be measured in dollars and cents, and this change is an adjustment. However, if you are results-oriented, and get results, you'll find the change interesting, even exciting.

Unfortunately, teachers who want to change jobs fear loss of income. Those apprehensions about taking a financial step backward seem to be the hardest hurdle for teachers to overcome. Yet, with a successful track record, former teachers recover an income loss in two to three years and can gain an additional $20,000 in five years. The income potential in business, industry, and sales is three times what it is in teaching. Anyhow, when you are free to choose what you want to do and really enjoy what you are doing, you find you can make it on less and that you wouldn't even consider taking a summer off.

Computer Operator

I am in a completely different field, in a completely different environment, from teaching. Yet I consider my teaching experience a plus. Through it I developed a greater degree of management ability, patience, flexibility—all helpful characteristics.

I had taught for five years—eighth grade math and science and one year of high school physical education. I began to take some computer classes before the layoff, and believe that doing so helped me get a new start. I was able to say that I had started a job-related program of study. I located my initial computer job through a personal contact. Currently I operate I/O machines (printer, card reader, card punch, mylar punch, FR 80) and serve as backup operator to senior console operators on two different systems. My career is progressing and I anticipate advancement to systems programming in the near future.

My advice is, don't be afraid to try something new, even if you don't feel you fully meet the qualifications specified. I found that some employers consider ex-teachers very desirable employees due to their experience in dealing with people and handling responsibility.

Supervisor, School Programs, Metropolitan Utility Company

In this position, I am responsible for supervising the development and implementation of educational programs for multi-disciplinary use by educators and students of all grade levels. In addition, I serve as a resource person and consultant to local, state, and national organizations responsible for developing educational policies and programs. We develop materials, both printed and audio-visual, give workshops, and do classroom presentations. Our presentations can cover any topics deemed appropriate for our utility company, such as energy, safety, economics, and career education.

Teaching skills I find valuable are my ability to work with a variety of personalities, to manage my time, to develop instructional materials, to coordinate many projects simultaneously, and to communicate well both orally and in writing.

I had taught social studies, history, and government for seven and a half years. I became aware of this opening through my involvement in a state professional organization for social studies. I enjoy new experiences and challenges, so I did an analysis of the skills I possess and, feeling confident, applied for the position. I was hired and later received the promotion to supervisor.

THE EXPERIENCE OF OTHERS

Analyzing personal skills seems to be hard for teachers to do. Even after completing an analysis, they seem to have little confidence in these abilities. I can tell you, those skills are valuable. Those skills, plus my confidence in them, have led me to my present position and responsibility for a six-figure budget.

Account Representative

I left teaching and gave up something that was good for something that I thought might be even better. That is usually a very difficult decision to make.

I had started teaching at age thirty-three and liked it. While I enjoyed teaching, I also wanted to create more options for a long-range career plan. A friend, who was an outside sales rep for a pharmaceutical company, was making twice as much as I in half the hours, and enjoying greater autonomy, a company car, and an expense account. That looked good!

I made a move into sales and now handle a half-million-dollar territory selling professional and commercial products in a metropolitan area. I am also a field sales trainer for the company.

Many teaching skills transfer to sales: motivational skills, written and oral communication skills, involvement with people, enthusiasm, public speaking, listening skills, problem solving. Selling is best achieved when the sales rep can help people solve their problems; teachers do this constantly.

Interestingly, after leaving teaching, I began to receive telephone calls from teachers wondering about career change. I gradually began to meet that need, did some research and writing, began conducting career change seminars, did some publishing and direct mail marketing, and now offer consulting services to schools. The opportunity looms ahead for yet another move, away from the corporation, as I expand operations as director of my own company.

If you are a teacher wanting a career change, you *can* relate your experience to other careers. My previous sales

ALTERNATIVE CAREERS FOR TEACHERS

experience, which opened the opportunity to become an account rep, consisted of *"developing, promoting, and delivering a communication skills package daily to 150 sometimes reluctant clients"* —for three years I taught English!

3.

PLANNING MAKES IT HAPPEN BETTER

If you want something to happen:
Imagine yourself doing it,
Make it a goal,
Make time for it,
Make room for it,
Make plans for it,
Build support for it;
Above all, *act* on it.

Having decided to work on a career change, consider and plan your course of action in advance. Planning provides greater assurance of success. In planning, you organize the facts in order to chart your course. Assessing your current situation objectively gives you the necessary facts. In the preliminary planning outlined here you will:

(1) Develop a timeline
(2) Evaluate your finances
(3) Develop support for your course of action

As you continue the career change process, you will gather more information and plan more steps toward a new career.

PLANNING FOR TIME

If you are facing possible layoff, then meet the problem head on. Find out exactly how much time you have until you'll need to be established in another career. Confront the personnel office and get any data you require. If you are not under an imminent deadline, set a reasonable time frame for yourself. Thus, you can do timely planning. You will need to budget for the following:

(1) Self-assessment (Chapter 4)
(2) Investigation of career alternatives (Chapters 5 and 6)
(3) Interviewing to gather information and to establish a network (Chapter 6)
(4) Development and preparation of a resume (Chapter 7)
(5) Target marketing of yourself (Chapter 8)

Provide yourself time by planning ahead. Establish a reasonable target date. Some teachers have used a full year, while still teaching, to market their skills into a new field. They approached it as they would a master's degree program that required evenings and weekends of work, study, meetings, and writing. Others used summer jobs or volunteer work done over a span of years to create a very gradual transition. Such long periods of time are not necessary, but a few months are far better than none. If you have little lead time available, accelerate the process. As Emerson said, "In skating over thin ice, our safety is in our speed."

Timing Tips

- If at all possible, begin preparation and searching while still employed. You are in a more positive ego state and can avoid errors induced by desperation. Employers also seem to prefer to interview and hire people who are already employed.

PLANNING MAKES IT HAPPEN BETTER

Searching while still employed indicates initiative and interest; still being on someone's payroll enhances your value and bargaining power.

- Are you asking yourself, "How will I ever do this while employed?" The only answer to the problem of not having enough time is to prioritize. Use your time for what is most important.

- Do not procrastinate. Procrastination is a behavior pattern that keeps you where you are. Choose action over inaction.

- Since the vast majority of jobs are found in the hidden job market (never advertised but discovered through word of mouth), plan time to tap this market. This will mean phone time, meeting time, letter and note writing time.

- As long as layoffs and burnout continue, there always will be a fairly large number of teachers seeking a career change in June. That number will swell dramatically after planned vacations and when the layoff notices of spring become the reality of September unemployment. Obviously, it is sensible to time your move, particularly your interviews for jobs, to avoid the peaks of competition.

PLANNING FINANCES

The financial implication of a career change is the bugaboo that most bothers teachers considering a move. This is especially true for those with eight to ten years of teaching experience and an advanced degree. Such a teacher, near the top of the salary scale, may anticipate a temporary loss in income. The key word, however, is temporary.

ALTERNATIVE CAREERS FOR TEACHERS

Earnings in business and industry are open-ended and confidential. One is compensated on the basis of merit and performance. Salaries do not peak after eleven or fifteen years, as in education, and it does not take as long for salary advancement to occur. Economic apprehensions need not stop you from a career change.

A 1980 follow-up study on graduates of the University of Michigan[1] who had received teaching certificates from 1946 through 1976, reported the income patterns of teachers and noneducators (recipients of teaching certificates engaged primarily in employment other than teaching). While educators who persisted in teaching reported a narrow range of salaries, primarily due to step-level salary schedules, the salary range reported by the noneducators was much broader, with 33 percent earning over $30,000. A substantial percentage (11.7) earned over $45,000 per year; none of the teachers reported salaries in this range.

Recent University of Michigan graduates (those receiving teaching certificates in 1970 or later) provided evidence of what has occurred in a rather restricted job market for teachers. These graduates sought alternative careers because they found teaching positions unavailable. Yet they have fared well. Their average income was found to be 12 percent higher than that of their teaching counterparts, and 7.4 percent reported salaries over $30,000. None of the teachers among recent graduates had achieved this income level. The "recent noneducators" also saw better prospects for advancement and were more likely to feel that their current positions offered sufficient status and prestige. They also perceived other opportunities, more frequently believing it possible to find another position with the same income and fringe benefits.

You may need to be flexible regarding salary and level of responsibility on the initial job. Then, as you learn about the company and its work, your college degree and teaching experience—those credentials and skills that are in your pocket—will facilitate your advancement. You can become aware of potential advancement by asking some searching questions about career

---

[1] Stark and others, "Teacher Certification," p. 3.

paths and promotional possibilities during your interviews. Salaries vary among regions of the country, industries, and fields within industries. Your own research will uncover the specific income realities for you within the options that you are considering.

While you may need to be flexible regarding salary and level of responsibility in a new career, only you can decide how flexible you can afford to be. Decide your actual income requirements for maintaining a reasonable lifestyle. Sort out what other alternatives exist for producing income. Is there a spouse willing to work, even temporarily? Are there savings available to carry you through a period of transition into a new career? Discover the real bottom line. You then have a figure to work with as a required minimum starting salary.

As you consider career options, investigate salary levels in initial positions and typical income levels further up those career paths. Ask some questions about typical "salary ranges" when doing information gathering and research. With that information in hand, realistically appraise your financial situation projected over a five- or ten-year period. The financial choices before you in career planning can then be viewed in the short term and long range.

Financial Tips

- Don't count on part-time work coupled with full-time employment outside teaching to supplement an initial salary. You will not have the time.

- Knowing your bottom line for survival does not mean that you have to accept that income.

- Incomes vary from industry to industry. The manufacturing industry has ranked highest in sharing profits with employees, followed by public service, wholesale and retail sales, and finally, financial institutions. Retail sales jobs, while often available part time, can be long on unusual hours and short on return benefits.

- Recognize that dollars can be taxed away and that a good fringe benefit package may allow you to bring home more of what you need. A good teacher's contract provides about an additional 25 percent in fringes over salary.

- If possible, take a leave of absence to make your career move. Faced with declining enrollments, some school systems have recently liberalized their leave policies to aid employees seeking a change and to avoid layoffs. Investigate the leave policy. Request a leave first; you can always resign later. There is no need to burn bridges behind you.

- Some jobs which promise the highest starting salaries—commission sales, real estate, and others—tend also to carry high risks. In them, you find a bomb timed by economic conditions. Many teachers have real estate licenses and have enjoyed benefits from sales work. With the state of today's economy, however, most are also glad they are teaching. Weigh risks as well as salary benefits.

MORAL SUPPORT/ STAYING POSITIVE

Some of your hurts you have cured,
And the sharpest you still have survived,
But what torments of grief you endured
From evils which never arrived!

Ralph Waldo Emerson

Maintain a positive attitude. It is essential that you feel good about yourself so that you act in self-enhancing ways. Being positive, enthusiastic, and optimistic is attractive to employers and to people who will help you. Feeling good about yourself is so very important because it enables you to radiate and communicate your worth.

Plan some strategies to provide yourself with moral support and to maintain your positive attitude. It is absurdly unfair to expect yourself to bat a thousand. Be realistic about the career change experience. You will face some rejection. Richard Nelson Bolles, in his now annually updated manual on career change entitled *What Color Is Your Parachute?*, talks about the numbers game and rejection shock. He reports that for every 245 resumes received by a number of different companies, an average of only one invitation to interview was extended.[2] When you experience rejection, understand that it is a result of the screening-out process used by employers to manage mountains of paperwork.

Tips for Staying Positive

- Do your own skill analysis, resume, and research following the suggestions in this book. By doing so, you will develop greater understanding of yourself and the career marketplace. Boost your own confidence, find your own direction, and acquire insights to aid you in gaining entrance to a new career path. No one else can do it for you. If you are waiting for your ship to come in, for someone else to unload it and drive the goodies somewhere for you, you will do just that—wait. Making it happen for yourself is far more enjoyable and much more effective.

---

[2]Richard Nelson Bolles, *What Color Is Your Parachute? A Practical Manual for Job Hunters and Career Changers* (Berkeley, CA: Ten Speed Press, 1984).

ALTERNATIVE CAREERS FOR TEACHERS

- Solicit support and understanding from your spouse or someone who is willing to offer encouragement and to keep you at the task of creating a career change. Share your goals, plans, and projected outcomes. Ask for the support you need. The most effective way to obtain something from another person is to ask for it. This is as true for emotional needs as it is for the physical needs. Yet we find it far easier to ask for the physical, like having the potatoes passed at dinner. Sharing an adventure multiplies the fun and brings close people closer together.

- Career alternative groups, people offering each other mutual support for career change, could be as helpful to you as they have been for housewives entering the job market. The successes also found in organizations like Weight Watchers and Alcoholics Anonymous and in group counseling demonstrate that support groups make it easier for individuals to try new behaviors and to follow through on commitments to themselves.

- Explore your community to see if any career change support groups exist. Check with your community college, the local adult education program, the university, or your local librarian, or tap the community agency referral system by placing a few strategic phone calls. Be wary of any which charge a large sum and offer grand promises. Your career change is yours to do. Own it.

- Start an "I am great" file to counter feelings of rejection prompted by your file of "Thank you, but . . ." correspondence. Put into the file anything that reflects nicely on you—awards, notes from parents or students, a copy of your evaluation, cards, letters of recommendation, evidence of accomplishment—anything that reminds you of what a great person you are. If you suffer from any rejection, browse through your "I am great" file and be reassured. This file can also be drawn from for ideas as you begin self-appraisal for your resume.

PLANNING MAKES IT HAPPEN BETTER

- Surrounding yourself with positive people makes it easier to stay positive. Consider the teachers' lounge. When crises hit a school system via layoffs, financial problems, negotiations, violence and aggression, or administrative problems, a shroud of gloom joins the cigarette smoke in the lounge. Those fellow teachers whose company you enjoy may be the least supportive people for you in your career change. Often the frustration of staff members is relieved in the lounge, among knowing and sympathetic listeners. Anger, negativism, and helplessness are expressed in conversations that "rehash the trash." When the trash really gets flying, it is hard not be hit. Recognize this and avoid getting caught in the negative thinking patterns of others. Surround yourself instead with positive people.

- Smile. The world looks much brighter from behind a smile and through eyes that sparkle.

People who experience trouble in their lives sometimes feel helpless, as if their situation is beyond their control. Feeling powerless, they stay in a rut. If you are troubled in your current career, that trouble is not an illness afflicting you or a condition caused by destructive forces outside. The trouble is a signal, a consequence, a call to action. Even trouble can be viewed in a positive way, as opportunity in workclothes.

ON PLANNING

As we conclude this chapter on preliminary planning, consider that planning can be a most valuable and effective procedure; it leads directly to organizing, coordinating, and ultimate success. But planning does not lead anywhere without action.

Some people plan and plan but never act. They are very busy—reading, thinking, analyzing, charting, striving to prepare

ALTERNATIVE CAREERS FOR TEACHERS

all the right moves. They spin their wheels most diligently; they go nowhere. Such planning becomes a form of procrastination.

Planning makes it happen better, but only action makes it happen at all.

4.

FINDING YOUR WAY

WHO ARE YOU? WHAT DO YOU WANT TO DO?

To make progress on a new career path, you need a sense of direction. This direction will evolve from knowing yourself and from understanding the world of work. You already have maturity, considerable education, and valuable experience. The task of understanding yourself and recognizing options is not as formidable for you, an adult, as it is for a student. Gathered within this chapter are exercises to aid your self-analysis. Like an artist choosing and mixing colors from a palette, you can choose from the data on these pages to create your own self-portrait.

Each of us is unique; no two people do a particular job in exactly the same way. The higher your legitimate level of skill, the less supervision you need, and the greater autonomy you receive to create your own career within a chosen field. This is as true outside education as it is in teaching. As a college graduate and an experienced teacher you are highly skilled. You thus will have considerable freedom in exercising your skills wherever you choose to use them. Your first task in developing your new career is gaining a better understanding of yourself.

ALTERNATIVE CAREERS FOR TEACHERS

SKILLS, TALENTS, ABILITIES, AND ACTION WORDS

The following three checklists are intended to aid you in identifying your skills, talents, and abilities. The first two lists describe skills. The last list contains action words that can be useful in highlighting skills, talents, and abilities.

These collections of terms have a number of uses. Doing the exercises at the end of the lists will aid you in discerning and labeling your skills.

Begin by using the checklists to identify the skills you possess.

Checklist of Skills, Talents, and Abilities

_____ accounted
_____ adapted
_____ adjusted
_____ administered
_____ advised
_____ analyzed
_____ announced
_____ anticipated
_____ applied
_____ appointed
_____ appraised
_____ approved
_____ arbitrated
_____ arranged
_____ assembled
_____ assessed

_____ assigned
_____ assisted
_____ audited
_____ authored
_____ bargained
_____ briefed
_____ budgeted
_____ built
_____ campaigned
_____ checked
_____ clarified
_____ coached
_____ collected
_____ communicated
_____ compared
_____ compiled

FINDING YOUR WAY

_____	composed	_____	explored
_____	computed	_____	facilitated
_____	conceptualized	_____	followed through
_____	conducted	_____	founded
_____	contacted	_____	graphed
_____	contracted	_____	grouped
_____	controlled	_____	guided
_____	constructed	_____	helped
_____	consulted	_____	hired
_____	coordinated	_____	implemented
_____	counseled	_____	improved
_____	critiqued	_____	improvised
_____	cut	_____	influenced
_____	decided	_____	initiated
_____	delegated	_____	installed
_____	delivered	_____	instructed
_____	demonstrated	_____	interacted
_____	designed	_____	interpreted
_____	developed	_____	interviewed
_____	diagnosed	_____	invented
_____	directed	_____	inventoried
_____	disciplined	_____	judged
_____	diverted	_____	launched
_____	drafted	_____	led
_____	economized	_____	lectured
_____	edited	_____	made
_____	enabled	_____	maintained
_____	encouraged	_____	managed
_____	enforced	_____	mediated
_____	enlightened	_____	motivated
_____	evaluated	_____	negotiated
_____	exchanged	_____	observed
_____	experimented	_____	obtained
_____	explained	_____	operated

ALTERNATIVE CAREERS FOR TEACHERS

- ____ ordered
- ____ organized
- ____ painted
- ____ patrolled
- ____ performed
- ____ persuaded
- ____ planned
- ____ prepared
- ____ prescribed
- ____ presented
- ____ prioritized
- ____ produced
- ____ programmed
- ____ promoted (as in public relations work)
- ____ proposed
- ____ proved
- ____ purchased
- ____ recommended
- ____ recorded
- ____ recruited
- ____ referred
- ____ related
- ____ reorganized
- ____ repaired
- ____ reported
- ____ researched
- ____ responded
- ____ reviewed
- ____ revised
- ____ scheduled
- ____ screened
- ____ served
- ____ set up (projects, limits, procedures)
- ____ simplified
- ____ sold
- ____ solved
- ____ spoke
- ____ staffed
- ____ streamlined
- ____ structured
- ____ studied
- ____ supervised
- ____ surveyed
- ____ synthesized
- ____ taught
- ____ tested
- ____ trained
- ____ treated
- ____ wrote

Checklist of Other Skills, Talents, and Abilities

- ____ artistry in (drama, dance, painting, etc.)
- ____ budget management
- ____ communication skill (verbal abilities)
- ____ computer literacy

FINDING YOUR WAY

- _____ craftsmanship in (carpentry, photography, stained glass, etc.)
- _____ debating
- _____ decision making
- _____ drafting
- _____ financial planning
- _____ forecasting
- _____ fund raising
- _____ group facilitating
- _____ journalistic ability
- _____ language fluency
- _____ leadership ability
- _____ listening skill
- _____ mentoring
- _____ modeling
- _____ musical ability (instrumental, vocal)
- _____ ombudsman ability
- _____ policy formation
- _____ problem solving
- _____ program development
- _____ public relations
- _____ public speaking
- _____ reasoning (scientific, numerical, mechanical, verbal)
- _____ troubleshooting
- _____ utilization of (technical equipment, community resources, etc.)

List of Action Words

accelerated _____
achieved _____
acted as _____
actively _____
appointed to _____
awarded (or was awarded) _____
completed _____
conversant in (languages or matters of) _____
cooperated in _____
delegated _____
detected _____
effected _____
eliminated _____

ALTERNATIVE CAREERS FOR TEACHERS

entrusted _____
established _____
expedited _____
fostered _____
generated _____
increased _____
inspired _____
knowledgeable _____
moderated _____
originated _____
oversaw _____
participated in _____
prevented _____
proficient in _____
promoted to _____
provided _____
reduced (costs, absenteeism, etc.) _____
reinforced _____
responsible for _____
resolved (conflict, problem, etc.) _____
restored _____
revamped _____
served as _____
shaped _____
significantly _____
stimulated _____
sought _____
successfully _____
supported _____
validated _____
won _____

Exercises for Examining Skills, Talents, Abilities, and Experience

- EXPERIENCE ANALYSIS One way to discover skills is to write a summary of your major accomplishments from various periods of your life. Identify skills employed in each accomplishment. Define any measurable outcomes that occurred.

- DISCUSSION Share your findings with someone who knows you. Your verbalizing will likely cause you to recognize more skills. The feedback will do so as well, and it may highlight skills that you tend to take for granted.

- PRIORITIZING Prioritize the skills you have identified. Which do you enjoy using? Which are your strongest? Which skills have you employed repeatedly? Which do you value most? Which would you like to use more in your next career?

- ARTICULATING Articulate your skills into the jargon of business and industry. Identify parallels. Anticipating the learning difficulties of students, for instance, relates to anticipating customer needs in preparation for a sales presentation.

- STATING SKILLS CONCISELY Use the checklist words to develop a list of good resume phrases that display your skills concisely. As you recall more experiences, add them to your list in effective phrases.

- INTEREST/SKILL ANALYSIS People work with data, people, things, or some combination of the three. Organize your skills according to involvement with these categories. Doing so will give you a start at clarifying your interests and, ultimately, the kind of work environment you will find most enjoyable. We tend to enjoy and find interesting those things that we do well.

ALTERNATIVE CAREERS FOR TEACHERS

PERSONALITY STRENGTHS

Hiring a good employee is like making a good marriage. A lot of personality is involved.

The list of personality strengths that follows could also be viewed as a list of self-management skills. While the previous list of skills focuses on interaction with areas outside of you—data, people, and things—this list focuses on the internal you, on your own style of management and living. Understanding yourself will help you relate your personality to various career options.

Check the personality strengths you possess. Additional exercises appear at the end of the list.

Checklist of Personality Strengths

_____	able	_____	artistic
_____	academic	_____	assertive
_____	accurate	_____	attentive
_____	active	_____	attractive
_____	adaptable	_____	bold
_____	adventurous	_____	broad-minded
_____	affable	_____	businesslike
_____	affectionate	_____	calculating
_____	aggressive	_____	calm
_____	agreeable	_____	capable
_____	alert	_____	caring
_____	ambitious	_____	cautious
_____	amicable	_____	charming
_____	analytical	_____	cheerful
_____	animated	_____	clear-thinking
_____	articulate	_____	clever

FINDING YOUR WAY

- _____ compassionate
- _____ competent
- _____ competitive
- _____ concise
- _____ confident
- _____ congenial
- _____ conscientious
- _____ conservative
- _____ considerate
- _____ consistent
- _____ constructive
- _____ cooperative
- _____ cosmopolitan
- _____ courageous
- _____ creative
- _____ curious
- _____ daring
- _____ decisive
- _____ deliberate
- _____ democratic
- _____ dependable
- _____ determined
- _____ dignified
- _____ diligent
- _____ disciplined
- _____ discreet
- _____ dominant
- _____ eager
- _____ easygoing
- _____ economical
- _____ effective
- _____ effervescent
- _____ efficient
- _____ emotional

- _____ empathetic
- _____ encouraging
- _____ energetic
- _____ enterprising
- _____ enthusiastic
- _____ ethical
- _____ exacting
- _____ expressive
- _____ fair-minded
- _____ faithful
- _____ farsighted
- _____ firm
- _____ flexible
- _____ fluent
- _____ forceful
- _____ formal
- _____ frank
- _____ friendly
- _____ generous
- _____ gentle
- _____ goal-oriented
- _____ good-natured
- _____ happy
- _____ healthy
- _____ helpful
- _____ holistic
- _____ honest
- _____ honorable
- _____ hopeful
- _____ humane
- _____ humanistic
- _____ humorous
- _____ idealistic
- _____ imaginative

ALTERNATIVE CAREERS FOR TEACHERS

- _____ independent
- _____ individualistic
- _____ industrious
- _____ informal
- _____ ingenious
- _____ inquisitive
- _____ insightful
- _____ intellectual
- _____ intelligent
- _____ intuitive
- _____ inventive
- _____ kind
- _____ leisurely
- _____ light-hearted
- _____ likable
- _____ logical
- _____ loyal
- _____ mature
- _____ methodical
- _____ meticulous
- _____ mobile
- _____ modest
- _____ motivated
- _____ natural
- _____ neat
- _____ nurturing
- _____ objective
- _____ obliging
- _____ observant
- _____ open
- _____ open-minded
- _____ optimistic
- _____ organized
- _____ original
- _____ outgoing
- _____ patient
- _____ peaceable
- _____ perceptive
- _____ perservering
- _____ persistent
- _____ personable
- _____ persuasive
- _____ pleasant
- _____ poised
- _____ polite
- _____ positive
- _____ practical
- _____ precise
- _____ productive
- _____ progressive
- _____ prudent
- _____ punctual
- _____ purposeful
- _____ quick
- _____ quiet
- _____ rational
- _____ realistic
- _____ reasonable
- _____ reflective
- _____ relaxed
- _____ reliable
- _____ reserved
- _____ resourceful
- _____ respectful
- _____ responsible
- _____ responsive
- _____ robust
- _____ secure

FINDING YOUR WAY

_____	self-assured	_____	thorough
_____	self-aware	_____	thoughtful
_____	self-confident	_____	tolerant
_____	self-controlled	_____	tough
_____	self-directed	_____	trusting
_____	self-reliant	_____	trustworthy
_____	self-starting	_____	unaffected
_____	sensible	_____	unassuming
_____	sensitive	_____	understanding
_____	serene	_____	unexcitable
_____	serious	_____	uninhibited
_____	sharp-witted	_____	unselfish
_____	sincere	_____	verbal
_____	sociable	_____	versatile
_____	spunky	_____	warm
_____	stable	_____	well groomed
_____	steady	_____	wholesome
_____	strong	_____	wise
_____	strong-minded	_____	witty
_____	sympathetic	Other:	
_____	systematic	_____	
_____	tactful	_____	
_____	talented	_____	
_____	teachable	_____	
_____	tenacious		

Exercises for Examining Personality Strengths

- ANALYSIS OF ACCOMPLISHMENTS Review the major accomplishments that you identified in the exercises on discovering skills. What personality qualities or self-management skills aided you in those successes? Have you checked all of them?

ALTERNATIVE CAREERS FOR TEACHERS

- PRIORITIZING List the ten personality strengths of which you are most proud. This will force you to be selective. Write why you value each trait; doing so will help you see their usefulness and hint at their marketability.

- DISCUSSION How would other people describe you? Share the list with people who know you or have them describe you in their own words. This exercise can generate valuable feedback. It may clarify and highlight personality strengths you underestimate or take for granted.

- RECOGNITION One way to demonstrate to a prospective employer that you possess these qualities is by offering letters of recommendation. When discussing skills and personality strengths, request letters of recommendation from those who recognize the qualities you possess. Sharing data from the exercises above may enable them to write more effective letters on your behalf.

    The most impressive demonstration of your personality strength occurs during personal contact with the people who will either hire you or lead you to the person who does. None of the paperwork of the job hunt can demonstrate the real you as effectively as you can in person. Would you think of arranging a marriage by mail? No! You would get out, play the field, learn about yourself and prospective partners, and then do some active courting. The same progression is involved in career change.
    If you feel uncomfortable being assertive and teaching others about yourself, it is time to change. Assertiveness will help you get the career you want. Your assertiveness will also make it easy for your employers to learn about the person they are hiring.

FINDING YOUR WAY

CAREER ENVIRONMENT OPTIONS

Other factors, besides skills and personality strengths, influence career choice. While skills focus on what you can do, and personality focuses on who you are, you need also to consider your preferences for work environments. By examining career environmental options and identifying those you want, you gain direction for your career search.

The world of work has been analyzed, sorted, and clustered in many ways. The function of most interest inventories is primarily to aid an individual in weighing his or her own preferences against the characteristics of career options. While such inventories can be helpful, one of the most effective devices for discovering an individual's career direction has simply been the question, "What do you want to do?"

Use this checklist of career environment options to identify those which appeal to you.

Checklist of Career Environment Options

Areas of Work

I prefer working in the area of:

ALTERNATIVE CAREERS FOR TEACHERS

_____ agribusiness and natural resources

_____ business and office

_____ communications and media

_____ construction

_____ consumer and home-making education

_____ environment

_____ fine arts and humanities

_____ health and medical

_____ leisure, recreation, and hospitality

_____ manufacturing

_____ marine science

_____ marketing, merchandising, and distribution

_____ personal service

_____ public service

_____ transportation

Work Activities

I prefer:

_____ data-oriented work

_____ people-oriented work

_____ things-oriented work

_____ computational work

_____ technical work

_____ persuading others

_____ artistic work

_____ literary work

_____ musical work

_____ social service work

_____ clerical work

_____ manual or physical work

_____ research

_____ scientific work

_____ creative work

_____ repetitive work

_____ varied work

_____ organized or systematic work

_____ not making decisions

_____ making decisions

_____ nondetailed work

_____ precise, accurate, detailed work

FINDING YOUR WAY

Relating to Others

I prefer:

_____ working alone, independently
_____ being supervised
_____ serving people directly

_____ working as a team member
_____ directing others
_____ serving people indirectly

I prefer interacting with:

_____ contemporaries
_____ older people
_____ enterprising people
_____ athletic people
_____ investigative, analytic, problem-solving people

_____ younger people
_____ a variety of age groups
_____ mechanically inclined people
_____ artistic, creative, and innovative people

Body and Clock Concerns and the Work Setting

I prefer work that is:

_____ fast paced
_____ slow paced
_____ unpressured
_____ sedate
_____ on a flexible schedule
_____ full time
_____ night time

_____ average paced
_____ pressured
_____ physically active
_____ on a regular schedule
_____ part time
_____ day time

I prefer work that:

_____ involves constant traveling
_____ involves no travel

_____ has some travel

ALTERNATIVE CAREERS FOR TEACHERS

I prefer a setting that:

_____ has a stable environment
_____ reduces interruptions
_____ is indoors
_____ is indoors and outdoors
_____ has noise
_____ is informal

_____ has a constantly changing environment
_____ provides interruptions
_____ is outdoors
_____ is quiet
_____ is formal

Values

I prefer doing work that satisfies my desire for:

_____ acceptance and belonging
_____ achievement
_____ affection
_____ approval
_____ authority
_____ being able to see results
_____ challenge and stimulation
_____ creativity, originality, and inventiveness
_____ companionship and interpersonal relationships
_____ competition
_____ emotional well-being
_____ future opportunities
_____ recognition and respect
_____ responsibility
_____ security

_____ fun and excitement
_____ health
_____ independence
_____ influence
_____ involvement and absorption in something of interest
_____ knowledge, mastery, and personal growth
_____ leadership
_____ mobility
_____ money
_____ power
_____ prestige and status
_____ stability
_____ variety

OTHERS:

_____

FINDING YOUR WAY

_____ self-expression _____

_____ skills _____

_____ service _____

Exercises for Analyzing Career Environment Options

- RATING Review the checklist of career environment options and rate each according to the following scale:

RATING	
1	most desirable
2	desirable
3	acceptable
4	undesirable
5	unacceptable

  Recognize both what you seek to obtain and what you seek to avoid within a new career.

- EXPERIENCE ANALYSIS Return to the descriptions of your major accomplishments. Analyze each to identify underlying preferences and interests involved in that work.

- DISCUSSION Share the results of these exercises with someone who knows you. The process of verbalizing and gaining feedback will clarify your interests. The feedback you receive can act as a catalyst for more thought.

ALTERNATIVE CAREERS FOR TEACHERS

PULLING IT ALL TOGETHER TO FIND A DIRECTION

Knowing yourself leads naturally to a sense of career direction because you will know what you seek in a new career. Self-awareness is essential. If you have a good sense of self, this next exercise will seem a very natural step.

Fill in the blanks using information collected about yourself. Do not worry if you do not have the information to fill in all the blanks. Your next goal will be to complete those blank sections by researching career options.

My Ideal Job

My ideal job would be to (job title or description) _____
_____
_____

using my skills of (work skills, personality strengths/self-management skills) _____
_____

in a work setting that included (career environmental options) ___
_____.

I want to earn _____ to start out and _____ within five years. I also want my new career to satisfy my desire for _____
_____.

It would especially intrigue or satisfy me if my work also involved (purpose, goals, life missions, personality dimensions—it's wide open) _____
_____
_____.

FINDING YOUR WAY

With heightened self-understanding, you now have a "wish list" in mind for your next career. Next you must discover what careers can fulfill those wishes.

5.

WITH YOUR CERTIFICATION, CONSIDER . . .

This chapter will suggest answers to the question, "What else can I do but teach?" It is meant to stir your imagination and stimulate interest in options—to provide you with a starting point in career exploration. Ignorance and apprehension limit choices. Begin now to broaden your view of where you can use your skills.

The job listings under each area of certification are not all-inclusive. To be included, each job had to meet the following criteria:

(1) First and foremost, the job draws on the knowledge and skills a teacher already possesses, thus requiring no additional training at your expense.
(2) The transitional possibility is realistic.
(3) The job has obvious potential for advancement and/or represents a professional position comparable to teaching.

As you evaluate the lists, keep in mind that job titles are one of the biggest blocks to job freedom. Different companies assign different titles to jobs requiring very similar skills. Some sales jobs are termed consultant jobs because the company perceives this to express more accurately the skills required—those of assessing clients' needs and offering suggestions or solutions.

WITH YOUR CERTIFICATION, CONSIDER . . .

Many of the positions listed under areas of certification are actually different jobs clumped under one title. *Personnel worker* is one such example. Today a person working in personnel in a large company could be specializing in training and/or orientation of employees, or interviewing, or developing a human resources program, or managing the benefits program of the organization, or working in the employee assistance program. Some companies have a broad view of personnel while others narrowly limit the functions of the department. Consequently, companies must be researched to determine which titles they use, the skills needed, and other job requirements. Job titles and stated requirements can vary dramatically from industry to industry, from company to company.

Listed at the end of each area of certification are addresses from which to request additional career information. Many of the organizations listed now require a nominal fee for this literature. Some of the information is excellent and well worth obtaining. If you are interested in a field, write the organization and request single copies of the free publications and a listing of career materials for which they charge a fee. You might also inquire if they solicit new members and about other services they offer, such as a journal or a placement service. Consider enclosing a large self-addressed stamped envelope to speed their response. Be sure to put your return address on the outside of the envelope as well as in the body of the letter.

Appendix I lists job opportunities within the government by college major. If you are interested in employment with the Federal Government, begin by contacting the Federal Job Center nearest you. Professional jobs are available but usually require many months to obtain. Do all the necessary paperwork or test taking for positions and then put your network to work and look for contacts in government employment. Networking is a valuable asset even in this sector.

Keep an open mind as you read the options listed under the certification areas. Read all the sections for which you are certified. Discover which options interest you. Think of other jobs, related to those that interest you, which are not listed. This chapter is only a starting point for a journey of discovery that can be exciting, challenging, and rewarding.

ALTERNATIVE CAREERS FOR TEACHERS

AGRICULTURAL EDUCATION MAJOR

A search for career alternatives can lead you in a variety of directions. Your knowledge of the multitudinous facets of agriculture, joined with your teaching experience, will provide excellent credentials for meeting the increasing information needs in agribusiness. While the Federal Government is a large employer, many industries that supply raw materials to farmers and process and distribute agricultural products also employ people in occupations that require agriculture-related training. Don't overlook possibilities in agricultural finance, communications, and exporting.

Investigate These Career Options

County Agricultural Agent (Government Service)

Organizes and conducts cooperative extension program to advise and instruct farmers and individuals engaged in agribusiness in applications of agricultural research findings. Collects, analyzes, and evaluates agricultural data, plans and develops techniques, and advises farmers in solving problems. Delivers lectures and prepares articles concerning subjects such as farm management, crop rotation, etc. May be designated by specific program assignment such as Agribusiness Agent, Farm Management Agent, Horticultural Agent, Livestock Agent, and Resource Agent.

Sales Representative, Poultry Equipment and Supplies (Wholesale)

Sells poultry equipment and supplies, such as brooders, coolers, feeders, graders, and washers. Advises customers on care and

WITH YOUR CERTIFICATION, CONSIDER . . .

feeding of poultry, setting up of poultry equipment, and egg production problems, and suggests remedial measures for diseased poultry.

Claims Adjuster

Investigates claims against insurance or other companies for personal, casualty, or property loss or damages and attempts to effect out-of-court settlement with claimant. Examines claim form and other records to determine insurance coverage. Inspects property damage to determine extent of company's liability.

Agricultural Commodities Inspector (Government Service)

Inspects agricultural commodities, processing equipment and facilities to enforce compliance with governmental regulations. Inspects horticultural products, such as fruits, vegetables, and ornamental plants to detect disease or infestations harmful to consumers or agricultural economy. Examines, weighs, and measures commodity. Writes reports of findings and advises grower or processor. May be designated according to type of commodity or animal inspected.

Soil Conservationist

Plans and develops coordinated practices for soil erosion control, moisture conservation, and sound land use. Conducts surveys and investigations on rural, agriculture, forestry, or mining measures needed to maintain or restore proper soil management. Applies principles of two or more specialized fields of science, such as agronomy, soil science, forestry, or agriculture, to achieve objectives of conservation.

Sales Representative—Farm and Garden Equipment and Supplies (Wholesale)

Sells farm and garden machinery, equipment, and supplies, such as tractors, feed, fertilizer, seed, insecticide, and farm and garden implements. May specialize in selling either machinery or supplies. Advises customers and makes recommendations.

Agriculture Market Research Analyst

Researches market conditions in local, regional, or national area to determine potential sales of product or service. Examines and analyzes statistical data to forecast future marketing trends and needs. Gathers data on competitors and analyzes prices, sales, and methods of marketing and distribution. Collects data on customer preference and buying habits. Prepares reports.

For Additional Career Information Write

Office of Personnel
U.S. Department of Agriculture
Washington, DC 20250

Farm Credit Administration   has information on careers
490 L'Enfant Plaza, S.W.   in agricultural finance
Suite 4000
Washington, DC 20578

Agricultural Director
American Bankers Association
1120 Connecticut Avenue, N.W.
Washington, DC 20036

Excellent sources of information are colleges and universities in your state that have agricultural curriculums.
Information on inspector careers in the Federal Government is available from State Employment Service offices or from Federal Job Information Centers located in various large cities throughout the country.

WITH YOUR CERTIFICATION, CONSIDER . . .

ART MAJOR

Your creativity and artistic ability provide you with career prospects that many cannot even consider. Assess your areas of greatest interest and expertise and explore options for careers in those areas. Opportunities exist for artists in publishing companies, museums and art galleries, fashion industries, advertising, and communications.

Investigate These Career Options

Merchandise Displayer

Displays merchandise, such as clothes, accessories, and furniture, in windows, showcases, and on sales floors of retail store to attract attention of prospective customers. Originates display ideas and constructs or assembles prefabricated display properties from wood, fabric, glass, paper, and plastic, using hand tools.

Interior Designer

Plans, designs, and furnishes interior environments of residential, commercial, and industrial buildings. Confers with client to determine architectural preferences, purpose and function of environment, budget, and other factors which affect planning interior environments. Selects or designs and purchases furnishings, art work, and accessories. Renders design ideas in form of paste-ups, drawings, or illustrations, estimates material requirements and costs, and presents design to client for approval.

Illustrator

Draws or paints illustrations for use by various media to explain or adorn printed or spoken word. Studies layouts, sketches of proposed illustrations, and related materials to become familiar with the assignment. Determines best style, technique, and medium to produce desired effects and conform with reproduction requirements, or receives specific instructions regarding these variables.

Sales Representative, Hobbies and Crafts (Wholesale)

Sells hobby and craft materials such as leather, leather-working tools, ceramic clay, paints, and model kits. Explains and demonstrates use of tools and materials to retail dealers.

Department Store Assistant Buyer

Aids buyer in connection with purchase and sale of merchandise. Verifies quantity and quality of stock received from manufacturer. Authorizes payment of invoices or return of shipment. Approves advertising copy for newspaper. May sell merchandise to become familiar with customers' attitudes, preferences, and purchasing problems.

Textile Designer

Originates designs for fabrication of cloth, specifying weave pattern, color, and gauge of thread, to create new fabrics according to functional requirements and fashion preferences of consumers. Sketches designs for patterns on graph paper, using water colors, brushes, pens, and rulers or prepares written instructions to specify details, such as finish, color, and construction of fabric.

Art Conservator (Museum)

Coordinates activities of subordinates engaged in examination, repair, and conservation of art objects. Examines art objects to determine condition, need for repair, method of preservation, and authenticity.

WITH YOUR CERTIFICATION, CONSIDER . . .

Photojournalist

Photographs newsworthy events, locations, people, or other illustrative or educational material for use in publications or telecasts, using still camera. Travels to assigned locations and takes pictures. Develops negatives and prints film. Usually specializes in one phase of photography, such as news, sports, special features, or works as a free-lance photographer.

Dental Ceramist

Applies layers of procelain paste or acrylic resins over metal framework to form dental prosthesis, such as crowns, bridges, and tooth facings, according to a dentist's prescription, using spatula, brushes, and baking ovens. Mixes porcelain paste or acrylic resins to color of natural teeth according to prescription.

Technical Illustrator

Lays out and draws illustrations for reproduction in reference works, brochures, and technical manuals. May draw cartoons and caricatures to illustrate operation, maintenance, and safety manuals and posters.

For Additional Career Information Write

American Textile
   Manufacturers Institute
Communications Division
Suite 300
1101 Connecticut Avenue, N.W.
Washington, DC 20036

request *There's A Career for You in Textiles*

Office of Museum Programs
Arts and Industries Building
Room 2235
Smithsonian Institute
Washington, DC 20560

ALTERNATIVE CAREERS FOR TEACHERS

Society for Technical
  Communications
815 Fifteenth Street, N.W.
Washington, DC 20005

Opportunity Coordinator   request *Jobs and Opportunities*
Writer's Digest School   *for Artists and Craftworkers*
9933 Alliance Road
Cincinnati, OH 45242

National Art Education Association
1916 Association Drive
Reston, VA 22091

BIOLOGY MAJOR

As a life scientist you have specialized knowledge regarding all aspects of living organisms with a particular emphasis on the relationship of living things to their environment. You also have acquired special abilities in making this sophisticated scientific information understandable to the general public. Jobs exist for you in technical sales and service and in testing and inspecting. Many of these opportunities are in the Federal Government and in research in business and industry (especially food products, drugs, and chemicals). Don't overlook the possibility that many companies in business and industry can capitalize on your teaching background.

WITH YOUR CERTIFICATION, CONSIDER . . .

Investigate These Career Options

Sales Representative, Chemicals and Drugs (Wholesale)

Sells chemical or pharmaceutical products, such as explosives, acids, industrial or agricultural chemicals, medicines, and drugs. Calls on customers, informs customers of new products, and explains characteristics and clinical studies conducted with the products. Promotes and sells other products manufactured by the company.

Environmental Analyst

Conducts research studies to develop theories or methods of abating or controlling sources of environmental pollutants, utilizing knowledge of principles and concepts of various scientific disciplines. May be designated according to aspect of environment in which employed, such as Air Pollution Analyst, Soils Analyst, Water Quality Analyst, etc.

Inspector, Industrial Waste (Government Service)

Inspects industrial and commercial waste disposal facilities and investigates source of pollutants in municipal sewage and storm-drainage system to insure conformance with ordinance and permit requirements. Extracts samples of waste from sewers, storm drains, and water courses for laboratory tests. Issues citations to apparent violators of sanitation code or water quality regulations.

Inspector, Agricultural Commodities (Government Service)

Inspects agricultural commodities, processing equipment, and facilities to enforce compliance with governmental regulations. Inspects horticultural products, such as fruits, vegetables, and ornamental plants, to detect disease or infestations harmful to consumers or agricultural economy. Collects samples of pests or suspected disease material and routes to laboratory for identification and analysis. Writes reports of findings and advises grower or processor. May testify in legal proceedings.

Biologist

Studies origin, relationship, development, anatomy, functions and other basic principles of plant and animal life. May specialize in research on a particular plant, animal, or aspect of biology. May collect and analyze biological data to determine environmental effects of present and potential use of land and water areas. May prepare reports.

Food Technologist

Applies scientific principles in research, development, production technology, quality control, packaging, processing, and utilization of foods. May specialize in one phase of food technology, such as product development, quality control, or production inspection, technical writing, teaching, or consulting. Conducts basic research and researches and develops new products.

For Additional Career Information Write

U.S. Environmental Protection Agency
Washington, DC   20560

Pharmaceutical Manufacturers Association
1155 Fifteenth Street, N.W.
Washington, DC   20005

American Institute of Biological Science
1401 Wilson Boulevard
Arlington, VA   22209

National Science Teachers Association
1742 Connecticut Avenue, N.W.
Washington, DC   20009

WITH YOUR CERTIFICATION, CONSIDER . . .

American Fisheries Society
5410 Grosvenor Lane
Bethesda, MD   20014

request *Career Guide 2000, Fisheries, Forestry, Wildlife and Related Occupations.* Send $3.00 for this guide on where jobs are, contacts for jobs, etc.

National Wildlife Federation
1412 Sixteenth Street, N.W.
Washington, DC   20036

request *Conservation Directory.* Send $4.00 to obtain up-to-date (published annually) list of agencies and organizations which deal with conservation.

BUSINESS EDUCATION MAJOR

As a business education major you possess skills and knowledge that can be applied in new career options. You have experience in instructing, motivating, evaluating, planning, organizing, and managing. You understand people needs as well as business needs and you use these insights daily to stimulate productivity and growth. Explore options in industry, business of all types, government and community agencies. You may wish to search for opportunities resulting from management's desire to involve employees in training programs designed to upgrade skills, increase productivity, and aid individual advancement.

ALTERNATIVE CAREERS FOR TEACHERS

Investigate These Career Options

Underwriter, Insurance

Reviews individual applications for insurance to evaluate degree of risk involved and accepts applications, following company's underwriting policies. Examines such documents as application forms, inspection reports, insurance maps, and medical reports to determine degree of risk from such factors as applicant's financial standing, age, occupation, accident experience, and value and condition of real property. Declines risks which are too excessive.

Sales Representative, Office Machines

Sells office machines, such as typewriters and adding, calculating, and duplicating machines, to business establishments. May sell office supplies, such as paper, ribbons, ink, and tapes. May provide training for individuals or groups who purchase new equipment. May rent or lease office machines. May be designated according to type of machines sold, such as Sales Representative, Cash Registers; Sales Representative, Bookkeeping and Accounting Machines, etc.

Credit Manager

Directs and coordinates activities of workers engaged in conducting credit investigations and collecting delinquent accounts of customers of commercial establishments, department stores, banks, or similar establishments. Investigates and verifies financial status and reputation of prospective customers applying for credit. Prepares documents to substantiate findings and recommends rejection or approval of applications. Reviews collection reports to ascertain status of collections and balances outstanding and to evaluate effectiveness of current collection policies and procedures.

WITH YOUR CERTIFICATION, CONSIDER . . .

Manager, Display

Develops advertising displays for window or interior use and supervises and coordinates activities of workers engaged in laying out and assembling displays. Consults with advertising and sales officials to ascertain type of merchandise to be featured and time and place for each display. Develops layout and selects theme, colors, and props to be used.

Instructor, Private Business School

Teaches business subjects to students in private business school. Organizes program of practical and technical instruction, involving demonstrations of skills required, and lectures on theory, practices, methods, processes, and terminology. Instructs students in subject areas. Plans and supervises work of students. Tests and evaluates achievement of students.

Sales Agent, Financial Report Service

Sells services, such as credit, financial, insurance, employee investigation reports, and credit-rating books to business establishments. Calls on establishments, such as financial institutions and commercial and industrial firms, to explain services offered by agency. Explains advantages of using impartial and factual reports and data as basis for assigning credit ratings, insurance, or security risks.

Claims Examiner

Analyzes insurance claims to determine extent of insurance carrier's liability and settles claims with claimants in accordance with policy provisions. Compares data on claim application, death certificate, or physician's statement with policy file and other company records to ascertain completeness and validity of claim. Corresponds with agents and claimants or interviews them in person to correct errors or omissions on claim forms and to investigate questionable entries. Pays claimants amount due.

ALTERNATIVE CAREERS FOR TEACHERS

Training Representative or Education Training Instructor

Prepares and conducts training programs for employees of industrial, commercial, service, or governmental establishment. Confers with management to analyze work situation requiring preventive or remedial training for employees. Formulates teaching outline in conformance with selected instructional methods, utilizing knowledge of specified training needs and of training effectiveness.

For Additional Career Information Write

American Society for Training and Development
P.O. Box 5307
Madison, WI   53705

Alliance of American Insurers
Public Relations Department
Room 2140
20 North Wacker Drive
Chicago, IL   60606

American Council of Life Insurance
1850 K Street, N.W.
Washington, DC   20006

Insurance Information Institute
110 William Street
New York, NY   10038

International Consumer Credit Association
243 North Lindbergh Boulevard
St. Louis, MO   63141

WITH YOUR CERTIFICATION, CONSIDER . . .

CHEMISTRY MAJOR

The majority of chemists are employed: (1) in government or industry to analyze or test products, (2) in technical sales or service positions, or (3) in research and development. Your teaching experience added to your academic knowledge will make you a valuable employee. Specifically, investigate drug companies, textile manufacturers, rubber and plastic companies, food industries, and chemical manufacturers. Be sure to read Appendix I in this book for government positions.

Investigate These Career Options

Sales Representative, Pharmaceutical Products

Promotes use of and sells ethical drugs and other pharmaceutical products to physicians, dentists, hospitals, and retail and wholesale drug establishments. Calls on customers, informs customers of new drugs, and explains characteristics and clinical studies conducted with drug. Discusses dosage, use, and effect of new drugs and medicinal preparations.

Market Research Analyst

Researches market conditions in local, regional, or national area to determine potential sales of product or service. Establishes research methodology and designs format for data gathering. Examines and analyzes statistical data to forecast future marketing trends. Gathers data on competitors and analyzes prices, sales, and methods of marketing and distribution. Prepares reports and graphic illustrations of findings.

ALTERNATIVE CAREERS FOR TEACHERS

Food Technologist

Applies scientific principles in research, development, production technology, quality control, packaging, processing, and utilization of foods. Conducts basic research and researches and develops new products. Studies methods to improve quality of foods. May specialize in one phase of food technology, such as quality control or production inspection. May specialize in particular branch of food technology, such as fats and oils, beverages, sugars and starches, preservatives, or nutritional additives.

Quality Control Technician

Tests and inspects products at various stages of production process and compiles and evaluates statistical data to determine and maintain quality and reliability of products. Selects products for tests at specific stages of production, and tests for items such as chemical characteristics. Records test data, using statistical quality control procedures, and prepares data in graph or chart form.

Colorist

Develops color formulas for printing textile and plastic materials and compares customer's sample with standard color card, or blends pigments into vinyl solution and compares results to determine formula required to duplicate color. Coordinates color shop activities with printing department production schedule. May inspect printed materials to insure adherence to plant specifications.

Water Purification Chemist

Analyzes water in purification plant to monitor chemical processes which soften it or make it suitable for drinking. Analyzes samples of filtered water to insure that quantities of solids left in suspension are below prescribed limits. Determines amounts of liquid chlorine to be used in chlorinators to destroy microbes and other harmful organisms. Tests samples extracted from

WITH YOUR CERTIFICATION, CONSIDER . . .

various points in distribution system, such as mains, tanks, pumps, and outlets, to discover possible sources of water contamination.

Malt Specifications Control Assistant

Keeps perpetual inventory of malt and barley in storage elevators and determines formulas for blending malt. Compiles continuous records of malt and barley supplies by location, amount, physical characteristics and chemical analysis. Analyzes physical and chemical test results to classify incoming barley shipments.

Chemical Laboratory Technician

Works in many industries conducting chemical laboratory tests and making qualitative and quantitative analyses of materials, liquids, and gases for purposes including research, development of new products and materials, health and safety standards, criminology, and environmental control. May analyze products, such as food, drugs, plastics, dyes, paints, detergents, paper, petroleum. May prepare chemical solutions for use in processing materials, such as textiles, detergents, paper, felt, and fertilizers, following standardized formulas or experimental procedures.

Yeast Culture Developer

Selects and cultivates yeast cells to develop pure yeast culture for brewing beer and malt liquors. Samples beer in fermenting stages to select specimens containing yeast cells having specific reproduction characteristics. Prepares coverglasses and slides with smears of yeast preparation taken from beer samples.

Food and Drug Inspector (Government Service)

Inspects establishment where foods, drugs, cosmetics, and similar consumer items are manufactured, handled, stored, or sold to enforce legal standards of sanitation, purity, and grading.

Visits specified establishments to investigate sanitary conditions and health and hygiene habits of persons handling consumer products. Collects samples of products for bacteriological and chemical laboratory analysis. Prepares reports on each establishment visited, including findings and recommendations for action.

For Additional Career Information Write

American Chemical Society
1155 Sixteenth Street, N.W.
Washington, DC   20036

Chemical Manufacturers Association
2501 M Street, N.W.
Washington, DC   20037

Institute of Food Technologists
Suite 2120
221 North LaSalle Street
Chicago, IL   60601

Pharmaceutical Manufacturers Association
1155 Fifteenth Street, N.W.
Washington, DC   20005

ECONOMICS MAJOR

As a major in economics, you have learned and refined research skills, problem-solving abilities, the techniques of compiling and analyzing data, and accuracy with detail. These skills, joined with your understanding of economic relationships, are important assets in such career areas as banking, insurance,

WITH YOUR CERTIFICATION, CONSIDER . . .

securities and investment, management consulting, economic research, and government service.

Investigate These Career Options

Loan Officer (Financial Institutions and Insurance)

Examines, evaluates, and authorizes or recommends approval of customer applications for lines or extension of lines of credit, commercial loans, real estate loans, customer credit loans, or credit card accounts. Analyzes applicant's financial status, credit, and property evaluation to determine feasibility of granting loan request. May supervise loan personnel. May handle foreclosure proceedings. May analyze potential loan markets to develop prospects for loans.

Sales Agent, Securities

Buys and sells stocks and bonds for individuals and organizations as representative of stock brokerage firm, applying knowledge of securities, market conditions, government regulations, and financial circumstances of customers. Gives information and advice regarding stocks, bonds, market conditions, and the history and prospects of various corporations to prospective customers, based on interpretation of data. Develops portfolio of selected investments for customers. Must obtain broker's license issued by state.

Budget Officer (Government Service)

Directs and coordinates activities of personnel responsible for formulation and presentation of budgets to implement federal program objectives. Directs compilation of data based on statistical studies and analyses of past and current years in order to prepare budgets and to justify funds requested. Prepares comparative analyses of operating programs by analyzing costs in relation to services performed during previous fiscal year and submits reports to director of organization with recommendations for budget revisions.

Insurance Underwriter

Reviews individual applications for insurance to evaluate degree of risk involved and accepts applications, following company's underwriting policies. Reviews company records to ascertain amount of insurance in force on single risk or group of closely related risks, and evaluates possibility of losses due to catastrophe or excessive insurance. Typically, workers who underwrite one type of insurance do not underwrite others, and are designated according to the type of insurance underwritten.

Appraiser

Appraises merchandise, fixtures, machinery, and equipment of business firms to ascertain values for such purposes as approval of loans, issuance of insurance policies, disposition of estates, and liquidation of assets of bankrupt firms. Examines items and estimates their wholesale or auction-sale values. Prepares and submits reports of estimates to clients, such as insurance firms, lending agencies, government offices, creditors, or courts.

Credit Analyst (Financial Institutions)

Analyzes credit data to establish degree of risk involved in extending credit or lending money to firms or individuals, and prepares reports of findings. Contacts banks, trade and credit associations, salesmen, and others to obtain credit information. Studies economic trends in firm's industry or branch of industry to predict probable success of new customer.

Claims Adjuster

Investigates claims against insurance or other companies for personal casualty or property loss or damages, and attempts to effect out-of-court settlement with claimant. Examines claim form and other records to determine insurance coverage. Inter-

WITH YOUR CERTIFICATION, CONSIDER . . .

views, telephones, or corresponds with claimant and witnesses. Prepares report of findings and negotiates settlement.

Credit Manager

Directs and coordinates the activities of workers engaged in conducting credit investigations and collecting delinquent accounts of customers on behalf of commercial establishments, department stores, banks, or similar establishments. Reviews collection reports to ascertain status of collections and balances outstanding and to evaluate effectiveness of current collection policies and procedures.

Financial Analyst

Conducts statistical analysis of information affecting the investment program of public, industrial, and financial institutions, such as banks, insurance companies, and brokerage and investment houses. Interprets data concerning investments, their price, yield, stability, and future trends. Summarizes data setting forth current and long-term trends in investment risks and measurable economic influences pertinent to the status of investments. May perform research.

Bank Officer

Manages branch or office of a financial institution, such as a bank, finance company, mortgage banking company, savings and loan association, or trust company. Coordinates activities to implement institution's policies, procedures, and practices concerning granting or extending lines of credit, commercial loans, real estate loans, and consumer credit loans. As a teacher with an economics major, you possess the skills for this position but may need to acquire experience through beginning management in the field.

Reporter

Collects and analyzes information about newsworthy events in order to write news stories for publication or broadcast. Receives assignment or evaluates leads and news tips to develop story idea. Gathers and verifies factual information regarding story. May specialize in one type of reporting, such as sports, fires, accidents, political affairs, or court trials.

For Additional Career Information Write

National Consumer Finance Association
1000 Sixteenth Street, N.W.
Washington, DC   20036

Security Industry Association
20 Broad Street
New York, NY   10005

American Bankers Association
Bank Personnel Division
1120 Connecticut Avenue, N.W.
Washington, DC   20036

American Council of Life Insurance
1850 K Street, N.W.
Washington, DC   20006

American Economic Association
1313 Twenty-first Avenue, South
Nashville, TN   37212

National Association of Business Economists
28349 Chagrin Boulevard
Suite 201
Cleveland, OH   44122

WITH YOUR CERTIFICATION, CONSIDER . . .

ELEMENTARY EDUCATION MAJOR

The wide variety of skills you have acquired through teaching can be used in other occupations. Occupations that use some or all of these skills are administrative officer, education and training manager for government or private industry, employment interviewer, newswriter, public relations representative, records manager, and sales representative. As an elementary school teacher seeking new career options, capitalize on your organizational and administrative skills, your power to influence, to motivate, and to train others.

Investigate These Career Options

Sales Representative, School Equipment and Supplies (Wholesale)

Sells school equipment and supplies, such as blackboards, art supplies, school furniture, etc. Calls on regular or prospective customers to solicit orders. May demonstrate products and point out salable features. Answers questions and advises customers. May specialize in certain product lines.

Personnel Manager

Plans and carries out policies relating to all phases of personnel activity. Recruits, interviews, and selects employees to fill vacant positions. Plans and conducts new employee orientation to foster positive attitude toward company goals. Keeps records of insurance coverage, pension plan, and personnel transactions, such as hires, promotions, transfers, and terminations. Prepares reports and recommends procedures to reduce absenteeism and turnover.

ALTERNATIVE CAREERS FOR TEACHERS

Nursery School Manager

Organizes and leads activities of prekindergarten children in nursery schools or for patrons in large department stores, hotels, or resort areas. Organizes and directs games and plans other activities for the children. May plan meals, refreshments, or snacks for children.

Sales Representative, Playground Equipment (Wholesale)

Sells amusement and sporting equipment, such as athletic equipment or playground equipment. Calls on regular or prospective customers to solicit orders. May be required to make presentations. May demonstrate product and point out salable features. May advise prospective customers.

Recreation Supervisor

Coordinates activities of paid and volunteer recreation service personnel in a public department, voluntary agency, or similar facility such as a community center, park, etc. Develops and promotes recreation program, including music, dance, arts and crafts, cultural arts, nature study, social recreation and games, or camping. Trains personnel and evaluates performance. Interprets recreational service to public and participates in community meetings and organizational planning. May work in team with administrative or other professional personnel to insure that program is well balanced, coordinated, and integrated with other services.

Loan Interviewer

Interviews applicants applying for mortgage loans. Interviews loan applicants to elicit information, prepares loan request papers, and obtains related documents from applicants, such as blueprints and construction reports. Forwards findings, reports, and documents to appraisal department. Informs applicants whether loan requests have been approved or rejected.

WITH YOUR CERTIFICATION, CONSIDER . . .

Training Representative or Education Training Instructor

Prepares and conducts training program for employees of industrial, commercial, service, or governmental establishments. Confers with management to analyze work situations requiring preventive or remedial training for employees. Formulates teaching outline in conformance with selected instructional methods, utilizing knowledge of specified training needs. Selects or develops teaching aids, such as training handbooks.

For Additional Career Information Write

National Education Association
1201 Sixteenth Street, N.W.
Washington, DC   20036

American Federation of Teachers
Fifth Floor
11 Dupont Circle, N.W.
Washington, DC   20036

American Society for Training and Development
P.O. Box 5307
Madison, WI   53705

American Bankers Association
Bank Personnel Division
1120 Connecticut Avenue, N.W.
Washington, DC   20036

ENGLISH MAJOR

One of your major strengths is your communication skill. You have command of the language (both written and oral), excellent vocabulary, and an analytical mind. You have been an editor for as many years as you have been teaching. As you begin your career search, examine opportunities where value is placed on your strengths. Consider careers in publishing, technical writing, public relations, advertising, sales, consumer relations, personnel, and government.

Investigate These Career Options

Reporter

Collects and analyzes information about newsworthy events to write news stories for publication or broadcast. Receives assignment or evaluates leads and news tips to develop story ideas. Gathers and verifies factual information regarding story through interview, observation, and research. May specialize in one type of reporting, such as education, foreign affairs, or community news.

Writer, Technical Publications

Develops, writes, and edits material for reports, manuals, briefs, proposals, instruction/textbooks, catalogs and related technical and administrative publications. Organizes material and completes writing assignment according to set standards regarding order, clarity, conciseness, style, and terminology. May assist in laying out material for publication.

Training Representative or Education Training Instructor

Prepares and conducts training programs for employees of industrial, commercial, service, or governmental establishment. Confers with management to analyze work situation requiring preventive or remedial training for employees. Formulates teaching outline, selects and develops teaching aids, and conducts new employee orientation.

WITH YOUR CERTIFICATION, CONSIDER . . .

Sales Representative, Publications (Wholesale)

Sells publications, such as books and periodicals. Suggests sales promotion techniques to retail dealers to increase sales. May represent publishing companies, and may specialize in educational textbooks.

Dictionary Editor

Researches information about words that make up language and writes and reviews definitions for publication in dictionary. Conducts or directs research to discover origin, spelling, syllabication, pronunciation, meaning, and usage of words. Organizes research material and writes dictionary definition.

Employment Interviewer

Interviews job applicants to select persons meeting employer qualifications. Reviews completed application and evaluates applicant's work history, education and training, job skills, salary desired, and physical and personal qualifications. May seek out potential applicants and try to interest them in applying for position opening.

Encyclopedia Research Worker

Analyzes information on specified subjects to answer inquiries from encyclopedia owners. Refers to library sources or consults with experts in field of knowledge involved. Prepares written summary of research findings for mailing to inquirers.

For Additional Career Information Write

American Society for Training and Development
P.O. Box 5307
Madison, WI 53705

ALTERNATIVE CAREERS FOR TEACHERS

American Society for Personnel Administration
30 Park Drive
Berea, OH 44017

National Council of Teachers of English
1111 Kenyon Road
Urbana, IL 61801

The Newspaper Fund, Inc.
P.O. Box 300
Princeton, NJ 08540

Society for Technical Communications
815 Fifteenth Street, N.W.
Washington, DC 20005

FOREIGN LANGUAGES MAJOR

Exciting possibilities exist for you in import/export businesses, banking, diplomatic services, journalism, broadcasting, international sales, and with international churches and social agencies (Red Cross, CARE, YMCA, adoption agencies). Your knowledge of a foreign language coupled with your understanding of foreign currency, culture, geography, history, and industries provides you with multiple job competencies. Consider, too, the many options available in the Federal Government.

Investigate These Career Options

Sales Agent, Franchise

Solicits purchase of franchise operation by contacting persons who meet organization's standards. Visits prospects to explain

WITH YOUR CERTIFICATION, CONSIDER . . .

advantages of franchised business, services to be rendered, costs, locations, and financial arrangements. May assist franchise purchaser in early stages of operating business. May work regionally, nationally, or internationally.

Interpreter

Translates spoken passages from one language into another. Provides consecutive or simultaneous translation between languages. Usually receives briefing on subject discussed prior to interpreting sessions. May be designated according to language or languages interpreted. May specialize in specific subject area.

Travel Agent

Plans itineraries and arranges accommodations and other travel services for customers of travel agency. Converses with customer to determine destination, mode of transportation, travel dates, financial considerations, and accommodations required. May specialize in foreign or domestic service, individual or group travel, specific geographic areas, airplane charters, or package tours by bus. May serve as guide for group taking foreign tour or domestic tour.

Foreign Banknote Teller-Trader

Buys and sells foreign currencies and drafts and sells travelers' checks, according to daily international exchange rates, working at a counter in a foreign exchange office. Gives information to patrons about foreign currency regulations.

Stenographer

Takes dictation in shorthand of correspondence, reports, and other matter. Performs variety of clerical duties. May take dictation in foreign language and be known as a Foreign Translator.

ALTERNATIVE CAREERS FOR TEACHERS

Correspondence Clerk

Composes letters in reply to correspondence concerning such items as requests for merchandise, damage claims, credit information, delinquent accounts, incorrect billing, unsatisfactory service, or to request information. Reads incoming correspondence and gathers data to formulate reply. May be designated Foreign Trade Services Clerk in a financial institution.

Airline Flight Attendant

Performs variety of personal services conducive to safety and comfort of airline passengers during flight. Greets passengers, verifies tickets, records destinations, and assigns seats. May be designated to fly international flights only.

Foreign Student Adviser

Assists foreign students in educational institutions in making academic, personal, social, and environmental adjustments to campus and community life. Evaluates student qualifications in light of admission requirements and makes recommendations relative to admission. Encourages and coordinates activities of groups which promote understanding of foreign cultures.

Foreign Exchange Code Clerk

Codes and decodes cables relating to foreign exchange transactions to facilitate foreign commerce through domestic banks. May translate decoded foreign language messages into English. May code and transmit outgoing messages by teletype. Employed in financial institutions.

Reporter

Collects and analyzes information about newsworthy events in order to write news stories for publication or broadcast. Receives assignment or evaluates leads and news tips to develop story idea. May specialize in one type of reporting, such as sports, fires, accidents, or political affairs. May be sent to

WITH YOUR CERTIFICATION, CONSIDER . . .

outlying areas or foreign countries and be designated a Correspondent.

Foreign Service Officer

Represents interests of United States Government by conducting relations with foreign nations and international organizations. Renders personal service to Americans abroad and to foreign nationals traveling to the United States. Issues passports to Americans and visas to foreigners wishing to enter the United States. May be designated according to basic field of specialization, as Consular Officer, Cultural Affairs Officer, Diplomatic Officer, Information Officer, or Public Affairs Officer.

Translator

Translates documents and other materials from one language to another. Reads and rewrites material in specified language or languages. May specialize in particular type of material, such as news, legal documents, or scientific reports and be designated accordingly. May be identified according to language translated.

Importer/Exporter

Exports domestic merchandise to foreign merchants and consumers and imports foreign merchandise for sale to domestic merchants or consumers. Arranges for purchase and transportation of imports through company representatives abroad and sells imports to local customers. May be required to be fluent in language of country in which import or export business is conducted.

For Additional Career Information Write

United States Information Agency
Office of Special Programs
Washington, DC 20547

ALTERNATIVE CAREERS FOR TEACHERS

Center for Applied Linguistics
1611 North Kent Street
Arlington, VA 22209

Modern Language Association
62 Fifth Avenue
New York, NY 10011

American Translators Association
109 Croton Avenue
Ossining, NY 10562

American Council on the Teaching of Foreign Languages
Two Park Avenue
New York, NY 10016

American Society of Interpreters
1629 K Street, N.W.
Washington, DC 20006

American Airlines, Inc.
Manager, Flight Attendant Recruitment
American Airlines Stewardess College
Greater Southwest International Airport
Fort Worth, TX 76125

Supervisor, Flight Attendant Recruitment
Eastern Airlines
Miami International Airport
Miami, FL 33148

Foreign Service
Staff Director
Board of Examiners
Department of State
Washington, DC 20520

WITH YOUR CERTIFICATION, CONSIDER . . .

GEOGRAPHY MAJOR

Opportunities for employment for those possessing a geography major are continually growing. Formal training in geography provides a background for a wide range of jobs, such as those available with manufacturing firms, insurance companies, government agencies, real estate development corporations, transportation planning companies, market research firms, in recreation, and with textbook and map publishers. Your abilities in problem solving, your effectiveness in communicating ideas both written and oral, and your interest in both the social and natural sciences will be an asset. Remember, many positions requiring a background in geography will not carry a geography title.

Investigate These Career Options

Cartographic Technician

Analyzes source data and prepares mosaic prints, contour maps, profile sheets, and related material. Prepares original maps, charts, and drawings from aerial photographs and survey data. Revises existing maps and charts and corrects maps in various states of compilation.

Sales Agent, Franchise

Solicits purchase of franchise operation by contacting persons who meet organization's standards. Visits prospects to explain advantages of franchised business, services to be rendered, costs, location, and financial arrangements.

ALTERNATIVE CAREERS FOR TEACHERS

Planning Aide

Compiles data for use by urban planner in making planning studies. Summarizes information from maps, reports, field and file investigations, and books. Traces maps and prepares computations, charts, and graphs to illustrate planning studies in areas such as population, transportation, traffic, land use, zoning, proposed subdivisions, and public utilities. May conduct field interviews and make surveys of traffic flow, parking, housing, educational facilities, recreation, zoning, and other conditions which affect planning studies. Usually employed by local government jurisdictions, but may work for any level of government or for a private consulting firm.

Sales Representative, Traffic Agent

Solicits freight business from industrial and commercial firms and passenger travel business from travel agencies and other organizations. Calls on prospective shippers to explain advantages of using company facilities. Quotes tariffs, rates, and train schedules. Explain available routes, load limits, and special equipment available and offers suggestions in method of loading, crating, and handling freight. Calls on travel agents and other organizations to explain available accommodations offered by the company. May specialize in soliciting freight or passenger contracts. May represent company in air transportation, motor transportation, railroad transportation, or water transportation.

Map Editor

Verifies accuracy and completeness of topographical maps from aerial photographs and specifications. Views photographs and other reference materials, such as old maps and records, and examines corresponding area of map to verify correct identification of specified topographical features and accuracy of contour lines. Examines reference materials to detect omission of topographical features, poor register, or other defect in photography or draftsmanship.

WITH YOUR CERTIFICATION, CONSIDER . . .

Immigration Inspector (Government Service)

Regulates entry of persons into United States at designated port of entry in accordance with immigration laws. Examines applications, visas, and passports and interviews persons to determine eligibility for admission, residence, and travel privileges in United States. Writes reports of activities and decisions.

Research Analyst

Researches market conditions in local, regional, or national area to determine potential sales of product or service. Establishes research methodology and designs format for data gathering. Examines and analyzes statistical data to forecast future marketing trends.

For Additional Career Information Write

Association of
  American Geographers
1710 Sixteenth Street, N.W.
Washington, DC   20009

request *Careers in Geography.*
Geography as a Discipline.
Geography: Tomorrow's Career

American Planning Association
1313 East Sixtieth Street
Chicago, IL   60637

request information on careers in planning

National Council for Geographic Education
University of Houston
Houston, TX   77004

American Congress on
  Surveying and Mapping
210 Little Falls Street
Falls Church, VA   22046

request information on careers in cartography

ALTERNATIVE CAREERS FOR TEACHERS

The Urban Land Institute
1090 Vermont Avenue, N.W.
Suite 300
Washington, DC 20005

GEOLOGY MAJOR

You are an environmental scientist who has studied the structure, composition, and history of the earth's crust. Openings for geology majors are expected to be better than average due to the world's search for petroleum and other new mineral sources.

Private industry is the largest employer of geology majors. They work in many capacities in petroleum companies, large construction corporations, mining, and quarrying companies. The Federal Government employs geologists in the Bureau of Mines, Army Corps of Engineers, Soil Conservation Service, and the Park Service. You also have the potential to be successful in many technical sales and service positions.

Investigate These Career Options

Laboratory Assistant or Petroleum Assistant

Tests sand, shale, and other earth materials to determine petroleum and mineral content and physical characteristics. Performs routine chemical or physical tests of earth samples in field or laboratory to determine content of hydrocarbon or other minerals indicating presence of petroleum and mineral deposits. Tests core samples brought up during well drilling to determine permeability and porosity of sample, fluid content of sand and shale, and other conditions affecting oil well drilling operations.

WITH YOUR CERTIFICATION, CONSIDER . . .

Lease Buyer (Mining and Quarrying; Petroleum Production)

Contacts landowners and representatives of other oil or coal production firms to negotiate agreements, such as leases, options, and royalty contracts covering oil or coal exploration, drilling, and producing activities. Discusses and draws up utilization agreements. Applies knowledge of company policies and local, state, and Federal laws relating to petroleum or coal leases.

Sales Representative, Oilfield Supplies and Equipment

Sells and rents oilfield supplies, machinery, equipment, and oil well services, such as directional drilling, electric well logging, perforating, and temperature and pressure surveying. May interpret graphs and survey data for customer.

Customs Import Specialist (Government Service)

Examines, classifies, and appraises imported merchandise and accompanying documentation according to import requirements, considering legal restrictions, country of origin, import quotas, and current market values. Requests laboratory testing and analyses of merchandise as needed. Notifies other governmental agencies when they are responsible for particular import inspection or when apparent import violations concern their regulations.

Inspector, Industrial Waste (Government Service)

Inspects industrial and commercial waste disposal facilities and investigates source of pollutants in municipal sewage and storm-drainage system to insure conformance with ordinance and permit requirements. Visits establishments to determine possession of industrial waste permits and to inspect waste treatment facilities, such as floor drains, sand traps, settling and neutralizing tanks, and grease removal equipment, for conformance with regulations. Extracts samples of waste for laboratory tests. Compiles written reports of investigations and findings.

ALTERNATIVE CAREERS FOR TEACHERS

Sales Representative, Petroleum Products (Wholesale)

Sells petroleum products, such as gasoline, oil, greases, and lubricants. May be designated according to specific petroleum product sold, as Sales Representative, Industrial Lubricants (wholesale).

For Additional Career Information Write

American Geological Institute
5205 Leesburg Pike
Falls Church, VA   22041

U.S. Office of Personnel Management
1900 E Street, N.W.
Washington, DC   20415

HISTORY MAJOR

As a history major, you most likely have strong analytic skills, training in research methods, good speaking and writing skills, and a high degree of intellectual curiosity. History provides lessons in cause-effect analysis. For a historian the development of skills in logic is as important as the broad knowledge of human experience. You have also acquired many additional skills through your teaching experience. The largest employers of history majors outside the field of education are libraries, museums, research corporations, government agencies, and historical societies and organizations. Historians with bachelor's degrees have for years been creative in career explorations. They have traditionally found that their inquisitive minds and research skills, coupled with some knowledge of business and/

WITH YOUR CERTIFICATION, CONSIDER . . .

or computers, make them valuable assets to business and industry.

Investigate These Career Options

Assistant Curator

Directs and coordinates activities of workers engaged in operating exhibiting institution, such as a museum. Directs activities concerned with instructional, acquisition, exhibitory, safekeeping, research, and public service objectives of institution. Assists in formulating and interpreting administrative policies of institution. Obtains, develops, and organizes new collections to expand and improve educational and research facilities. May participate in research activities.

Research Assistant

Conducts research on historic monuments, buildings, and scenes to reconstruct for exhibit. Collects information from libraries, museums, and art institutes. Monitors construction to insure authenticity. May write reports on findings. May work for large museums, historical society, social science research firms, government agencies, or other organizations.

Biographer

Specializes in reconstruction in narrative form of career or life of an individual. Assembles biographical material from sources, such as news accounts, diaries, personal papers and correspondence, and from consultation with associates and relatives of subject. May serve as consultant, or work in research and educational organization, or publishing firm.

ALTERNATIVE CAREERS FOR TEACHERS

Director, Historical Society

Directs activities of historical society. Reviews publications and exhibits prepared by staff prior to public release in order to insure historical accuracy of presentations. Speaks before various groups, organizations, and clubs to promote society's aims and activities. Consults with or advises other individuals on historical authenticity of various materials. May edit society publications. May conduct campaigns to raise funds for society programs and projects.

Archivist

Appraises and edits permanent records and historically valuable documents, participates in research activities based on archival materials, and directs safekeeping of archival documents and materials. Analyzes documents, such as government records, minutes of corporate board meetings, letters from famous persons, and charters of nonprofit foundations, by ascertaining date of writing, author, or recipient, in order to appraise value to posterity or to employing organization. Selects and edits documents for publication and display.

Travel Agent

Plans itineraries and arranges accommodations and other travel services for customers of travel agency. Plans, describes, and sells itinerary for package tours. Computes cost of travel and accommodations. May specialize in foreign or domestic service, individual or group travel, particular geographic area, airplane charters, or packaged tours by bus. May act as wholesaler and assemble tour package. May serve as tour leader.

Sales Agent, Insurance

Sells insurance to new and present clients, recommending amount and type of coverage based on analysis of prospect's circumstances. Contacts prospects and explains features and merits of policies offered. Calculates and quotes premium rates for recommended policies. Must have license issued by state.

WITH YOUR CERTIFICATION, CONSIDER . . .

For Additional Career Information Write

American Historical Association
400 A Street, S.E.
Washington, DC   20003

National Trust for Historic Preservation
1785 Massachusetts Avenue, N.W.
Washington, DC   20036

Organization of American Historians
Indiana University
112 North Bryan Street
Bloomington, IN   47401

Office of Museum Programs
Arts and Industries Building
Room 2235
Smithsonian Institution
Washington, DC   20560

HOME ECONOMICS MAJOR

This is an academic major that provides you with lots of avenues to explore. Check out employment opportunities in the Federal Government, with manufacturing companies (large and small appliances and food manufacturers), with utility companies and large financial institutions, and with pattern, notion and textile companies. Home Economists also work in the publishing industry—magazines, newspapers, and TV. Many are self-employed; they have perceived a need and created a service or business to meet that need.

Investigate These Career Options

4-H Club Agent

Organizes and directs educational projects and activities of 4-H Club. Recruits and trains volunteer leaders to plan and guide 4-H Club program to meet needs and interests of individuals and community. Procures, develops, distributes, and presents teaching materials, such as visual aids and literature for educational projects.

Interior Designer

Plans, designs, and furnishes interior environments of residential, commercial, and industrial buildings. Confers with clients to determine architectural preferences, purpose and function of environment, budget, and other factors which affect planning of interior environments. Advises clients on interior design factors, such as space planning, layout and utilization of furnishings and equipment, color schemes and color coordination. May specialize in particular field, style, or phase of interior design.

Sales Agent, Real Estate

Rents, buys, and sells property for clients on a commission basis. Studies property listings to become familiar with properties for sale. Interviews prospective clients to solicit listings. Accompanies prospects to property sites, quotes purchase price, describes features, and discusses conditions of sale or terms of lease.

Home Service Representative

Organizes and conducts consumer education service or research program for equipment, food, textile, or utility company, utilizing principles of home economics. Advises homemakers in selection and utilization of household equipment, food, and clothing, and interprets homemakers' needs to manufacturers of household products. Teaches improved homemaking practices

WITH YOUR CERTIFICATION, CONSIDER . . .

to homemakers and youths through educational programs, demonstrations, discussions, and home visits.

Manufacturer's Sales Representative for Clothes (Wholesale)

Sells women's and girl's apparel, such as coats, dresses, lingerie, and accessories, utilizing knowledge of fabrics, styles and prices. Performs other duties associated with a sales representative. May specialize according to price range of garment sold.

Tester, Food Products

Develops, tests, and promotes various types of food products. Selects recipes from conventional cookbooks, or develops new recipes for company food products. Evaluates prepared item as to texture, appearance, flavor, and nutritional value. Suggests new products, product improvements, and promotions for company use or for resale to dealers, manufacturers, or other users. Answers consumer mail.

Cooperative Extension Service Worker (Government Service)

Develops, organizes, and conducts programs for individuals in rural communities to improve farm and family life. Lectures and demonstrates techniques in such subjects as nutrition, clothing, home management, home furnishings, and child care. Organizes and advises clubs, and assists in selecting and training leaders to guide group discussions and demonstrations. Writes leaflets and articles. Talks over radio and television to disseminate information.

Merchandise Manager

Formulates merchandising policies and coordinates merchandising activities in wholesale or retail establishment. Determines mark-up and mark-down percentages necessary to insure profit, based on estimated budget, profit goals, and average rate of stock turnover. Determines amount of merchandise to be stocked and directs buyers in purchase of supplies for resale. Consults with other personnel to plan sales promotion program.

Assistant Buyer

Aids buyer in purchase and sale of merchandise. Verifies quantity and quality of stock received from manufacturer. Authorizes payment of stock received from manufacturer. Approves advertising copy for newspapers. May sell merchandise to become familiar with customers' attitudes, preferences, and purchasing problems.

Patternmaker

Draws sets of master patterns for garments or other articles, following sketches, samples, and design specifications. Examines sketches or sample articles and design specifications to ascertain number, shape, and size of pattern parts and quantity of cloth required to make finished article, using knowledge of manufacturing process and characteristics of fabrics.

For Additional Career Information Write

American Home
   Economics Association
2010 Massachusetts Avenue, N.W.
Washington, DC 20036

request listing of AHEA career publications

Home Economists in Business
301 Maple Avenue West
Tower Suite 505
Vienna, VA 22180

request *HEIB Directory*

National Association of Extension Home Economists
S.T.P. Building, Suite 207
953 East Sahara Avenue
Las Vegas, NV 89104

WITH YOUR CERTIFICATION, CONSIDER . . .

Sales and Marketing Executives International
380 Lexington Avenue
New York, NY 10017

INDUSTRIAL ARTS MAJOR

The varied components that comprise a major in industrial arts also provide numerous paths to explore. There are a multitude of sales jobs, wholesale or retail, which could use your knowledge and communication skills. There are also positions in business and industry for which you would be a good candidate due to your ability to manage, motivate, and organize, and to your knowledge of the tools of the trade.

Investigate These Career Options

Claims Adjuster

Investigates claims against insurance or other companies for personal, casualty, or property loss or damages and attempts to effect out-of-court settlement with claimant. Examines claim form and other records to determine insurance coverage. May be designated according to type of claim adjusted, as Automobile Insurance Claims Adjuster, Fire Insurance Claims Adjuster, Marine Insurance Claims Adjuster.

Construction Inspector

Inspects installations for conformance to safety laws and regulations and approved plans and specifications. Will be designated according to area of expertise, such as Building Inspector,

ALTERNATIVE CAREERS FOR TEACHERS

Electrical Inspector, Plumbing Inspector, Heating and Refrigeration Inspector.

Drafter

Draws rough layout and sketches, and assigns work to and directs subordinate drafting workers. Sketches layout according to design proposal and standard specifications and practices. Assigns drafting or detail drawings to subordinate personnel and verifies accuracy and completeness of finished drawings.

Sales Representative, Educational Courses

Solicits applications for enrollment in technical, commercial, and industrial schools. Contacts prospects, explains courses offered by school, and quotes fees. Advises prospective students on selection of courses based on their educational and vocational objectives. Compiles registration information.

Technical Illustrator

Lays out and draws illustrations for reproduction in reference works, brochures, and technical manuals dealing with assembly, installation, operation, maintenance, and repair of machines, tools, and equipment. Prepares drawings from blueprints, designs, mockups, and photoprints by methods and techniques suited to specific reproduction process or final use.

Sales Representative, Welding Equipment

Sells welding equipment, materials, and supplies to machine shops and other industrial establishments, utilizing knowledge of tool-and-die making, welding techniques, and metalworking processes.

WITH YOUR CERTIFICATION, CONSIDER . . .

For Additional Career Information Write

Alliance of American Insurers
Public Relations Department
Room 2140
20 North Wacker Drive
Chicago, IL 60606

send self-addressed, stamped
envelope with request
for career information

American Industrial Arts Association
1201 Sixteenth Street, N.W.
Washington, DC 20036

Society for
  Technical Communication
815 Fifteenth Street, N.W.
Washington, DC 20005

send self-addressed, stamped
envelope with request for
information on technical
illustrating as a career

JOURNALISM MAJOR

The art of communicating is as old as humanity, and is as important now as ever. Your acute powers of observation, your ability to think clearly and logically, your command of the language and feeling for choice of words will be beneficial to you and your search for a new career. Consider using free-lance work as a means of building a portfolio.

Investigate These Career Options

Columnist/Commentator

Analyzes news and writes column or commentary, based on personal knowledge and experience with the subject matter, for publication or broadcast. Gathers information and develops perspective on subject through research, interview, experience, and attendance at functions. Analyzes and interprets information to formulate and outline story idea. Selects material most pertinent to presentation and organizes into acceptable medium and format.

Public Relations Representative

Plans and conducts public relations program designed to create and maintain favorable public image for employer or client. Plans and directs development and communication of information designed to keep public informed of employer's programs, accomplishments, or point of view. Prepares and distributes fact sheets, news releases, photographs, scripts, motion pictures, etc., to persons who may be interested in learning about or publicizing employers' activities or message. May specialize in disseminating facts and information about organization's activities or governmental agency's programs to the general public and be known as a Public Information Officer.

Technical Writer

Develops, writes, and edits material for reports, manuals, briefs, proposals, instruction books, catalogs, and related technical and administrative publications concerned with work methods and procedures. Interviews production and engineering personnel and reads journals, reports, and other material to become familiar with product technologies and production methods. Organizes material and completes writing assignment according to set standard regarding order, clarity, conciseness, style, and terminology.

Reporter

Collects and analyzes information about newsworthy events in order to write news stories for publication or broadcast. Receives assignments or evaluates leads and news tips to develop story idea. Gathers and verifies factual information regarding story through interview, observation, and research. Organizes

WITH YOUR CERTIFICATION, CONSIDER . . .

material, determines slant or emphasis, and writes story according to prescribed editorial style and format standards.

Copywriters

Writes advertising copy for use by publication or broadcast media to promote sale of goods and services. Consults with sales media and marketing representatives to obtain information on product or service and to discuss style and length of copy. May write articles, bulletins, sales letters, speeches, and other related informative and promotional material.

Market Research Analyst

Establishes research methodology and designs format for data gathering by surveys, opinion polls, or questionnaires. Examines and analyzes statistical data to forecast future marketing trends. Gathers data on competitors. Collects data on customer preference and buying habits. Prepares reports.

Newswriter or Rewriter

Writes news stories for publication or broadcast from written or recorded notes supplied by the reporting staff. Reviews and evaluates notes to isolate pertinent facts and details. Verifies accuracy of facts and obtains supplemental material and additional details from files, reference libraries, and interviews with knowledgeable sources. Organizes material and writes story.

For Additional Career Information Write

Career Information
Public Relations Society of America, Inc.
845 Third Avenue
New York, NY 10022

ALTERNATIVE CAREERS FOR TEACHERS

The Newspaper Fund, Inc.
P.O. Box 300
Princeton, NJ 08540

American Newspaper
　Publishers Association
　Foundation
Newspaper Center
Box 17407
Dulles International Airport
Washington, DC 20041

request career information
and *Your Future in
Daily Newspapers*

Opportunity Coordinator
Writer's Digest School
9933 Alliance Road
Cincinnati, OH 45242

request *Jobs and
Opportunities for Writers*

Women in Communications, Inc.
P.O. Box 9561
Austin, TX 78766

LIBRARY SCIENCE MAJOR

Librarians play an important role in the transfer of knowledge and ideas by providing people with access to the information they want and need. Many positions are open outside public (K–12) education for persons possessing a library science degree. Employment opportunities exist in public libraries, college and university libraries, and in special libraries maintained in various areas of business and industry. Your highly developed skills of organizing and classifying data can be an asset in many careers. Jobs requiring similar analytical, organizational, and communicative skills include archivists, information scientists, museum curators, publishers' representatives, research analysts, information brokers, book critics, and records managers.

WITH YOUR CERTIFICATION, CONSIDER . . .

Investigate These Career Options

Special Librarian

Manages library or section containing specialized materials for industrial, commercial, or governmental organizations, for major newspapers, or for institutions such as hospitals. Selects, orders, catalogs, and classifies special collections of technical books, periodicals, manufacturers' catalogs and specifications, slides, films, etc. May be designated according to subject matter, specialty of library, or department, as Art Librarian, Business Librarian, Engineering Librarian, Law Librarian, Map Librarian, Medical Librarian.

Acquisition Librarian

Selects and orders books, periodicals, films, and other materials for large library. Reviews publishers' announcements and catalogs, and compiles list of publications to be purchased. Circulates selection lists to branches and departments for comments. May recommend acquisition of materials from individuals or organizations or by exchange with other libraries.

Bibliographer

Compiles lists of books, periodicals, articles, and audio-visual materials on particular subjects. Annotates bibliographies with physical description and analysis of subject content of materials. Recommends acquisition of materials in specialized subjects.

Publisher's Representative (Wholesale)

Sells publications such as books and periodicals. Suggests sales promotion techniques to retail dealers to increase sales. Performs other duties normally associated with a sales representative position.

ALTERNATIVE CAREERS FOR TEACHERS

Archivist

Appraises and edits permanent records and historically valuable documents, participates in research activities based on archival materials and directs safekeeping of archival documents and materials. Directs activities of workers engaged in cataloging and safekeeping of valuable materials and directs disposition of worthless materials. Directs filing and cross-indexing of selected documents in alphabetical and chronological order.

Information Scientist

Develops and designs methods and procedures for collecting, organizing, interpreting, and classifying information for input into a computer for retrieval. May specialize in specific field of information science such as business, medicine, education, or library science.

Encyclopedia Research Worker

Analyzes information on specified subjects to answer inquiries from encyclopedia owners. Refers to library sources or consults with experts in the field involved. Prepares written summary of research findings for mailing to inquirers.

Book Critic

Writes critical reviews of literary works. Reads books, analyzes factors such as theme, expression, and technique, and makes comparisons to other works and standards. Forms critical opinions based on knowledge, judgment, and personal experience. Organizes material to emphasize prominent features and writes review.

WITH YOUR CERTIFICATION, CONSIDER . . .

For Additional Career Information Write

Special Librarians Association
235 Park Avenue South
New York, NY 10003

American Society for Information Science
1010 Sixteenth Street, N.W.
Washington, DC 20036

American Library Association
50 East Huron Street
Chicago, IL 60611

MATHEMATICS MAJOR

Your ability to work with and understand abstract concepts is transferable to many careers. Persons trained in math are employed in all sectors of the economy including private industry, government, and colleges and universities. If you have acquired knowledge of computers, be certain to consider the many applications of computer science.

Investigate These Career Options

Actuary

Applies knowledge of mathematics, probability, statistics, principles of finance and business to problems in life, health, social, and casualty insurance, and in annuities and pensions. Determines mortality, accident, sickness, disability, and retirement rates. Constructs probability tables. Designs or reviews insurance and pension plans and calculates premiums. May specialize in one type of insurance.

Statistician

Conducts research into mathematical theories and proofs that form basis of science of statistics. Develops and tests experimental designs, sampling techniques, and analytical methods, and prepares recommendations concerning their utilization in statistical surveys, experiments, and tests.

Loan Counselor

Analyzes loan contracts and attempts to obtain payment of overdue installments. Studies records of delinquent accounts and contacts borrower to discuss payment due. Analyzes financial problems of borrower and adjusts loan agreement to restore loan to good standing. May be called upon to testify at legal proceedings.

Operations Research Analyst

Conducts analyses of management and operational problems and formulates mathematical or simulation models of problem for solution by computers or other methods. Analyzes problem in terms of management information and conceptualizes and defines problem. Prepares model of problem in form of one or several equations that relate constants and variables, restrictions, alternatives, conflicting objectives, and their numerical parameters. Prepares reports to management defining problem, evaluation, and possible solution. May work in association with engineers, scientists, and management personnel in business, government, health, transportation, energy, manufacturing, environmental sciences, or other technologies.

Sales Representative, Computers and EDP Systems (Wholesale)

Sells computers and electronic data processing systems to business or industrial establishments. Analyzes customer's

WITH YOUR CERTIFICATION, CONSIDER . . .

needs and recommends computer system that best meets customer's requirements. Emphasizes salable features, such as flexibility, cost, capacity, and economy of operation. Consults with staff engineers on highly technical problems. Performs other tasks normally associated with Sales Representative position.

Financial Analyst

Conducts statistical analyses of information affecting investment program of public, industrial, and financial institutions, such as banks, insurance companies, and brokerage and investment houses. Interprets data concerning investments, their price, yield, stability, and future trends, using daily stock and bond reports, financial periodicals, securities manuals, and personal interviews.

Insurance Underwriter

Reviews individual applications for insurance to evaluate degree of risk involved and accepts applications, following company's underwriting policies. Reviews company records to ascertain amount of insurance in force on single risk or group of closely related risks. Typically, workers who underwrite one type of insurance do not underwrite others, and are designated according to type of insurance underwritten, as Fire Underwriter, Liability Underwriter, Compensation Underwriter, etc.

For Additional Career Information Write

Mathematical Association of America
1529 Eighteenth Street, N.W.
Washington, DC   20036

American Mathematical Society
P.O. Box 6248
Providence, RI   02940

ALTERNATIVE CAREERS FOR TEACHERS

American Bankers Association
Bank Personnel Division
1120 Connecticut Avenue, N.W.
Washington, DC 20036

Society of Actuaries
208 South LaSalle Street
Chicago, IL 60604

American Council of Life Insurance
1850 K Street, N.W.
Washington, DC 20006

MUSIC EDUCATION MAJOR

A good music teacher possesses the same skills and aptitudes as other good teachers, and some in increased measure. Capitalize on your special ability to motivate groups, your generous portion of patience, your willingness to work long hours, your experience of performing before audiences, and your talent for viewing things independently while seeing vividly their relationship to the whole. If you choose to make music an avocation, you will still retain these skills. If you choose to continue music as your vocation, learn about opportunities in music publishing companies, record companies, music departments of TV and radio stations, and the Armed Forces.

WITH YOUR CERTIFICATION, CONSIDER . . .

Investigate These Career Options

Sales Representative, Musical Instruments and Accessories

Sells brass, percussion, stringed, and woodwind musical instruments, accessories, and supplies. Discusses effect of instrument construction on tone and quality. May appraise instruments for trade-in allowance. May rent instruments to customers and prepare rental contracts. May be sales representative for wholesale instruments and accessories, thus having somewhat different duties than stated above.

Private Music Teacher

Teaches individuals or groups instrumental or vocal music in home or place of employment. Plans lessons based on individual needs. Instructs students in music theory, harmony, score and sight reading, composition, and appreciation.

Instrument Repairer

Repairs, cleans, and alters brass and woodwind musical instruments. Inspects instruments, moves mechanical parts, or plays scale to determine defects. Makes necessary repairs.

Director of Fund Raising

Directs and coordinates solicitation and disbursements of funds for community social-welfare organizations, charities, or other causes. Establishes fund-raising goals according to financial need of agency. Formulates policies for collecting contributions.

Assistant Director, Music

Plans and directs activities of personnel in studio music department and conducts studio orchestra. Selects vocal, instrumental, and recorded music suitable to type of program or motion picture. Auditions and selects vocal and instrumental talent for musical shows. Auditions and hires studio orchestra personnel.

ALTERNATIVE CAREERS FOR TEACHERS

Sales Representative, Sheet Music

Sells books and sheet music for instrumental and vocal groups or for publishing companies, utilizing knowledge of composers, compositions, and types of music, such as classical, popular, and sacred.

Booking Manager

Books performers, theatrical or ballet productions, variety or nightclub acts, concerts or lecture series, or other popular or classical attractions for entertainment in various establishments, such as theaters, showplaces, and concert auditoriums. Negotiates with booking representatives or producers of attractions to arrange terms of contract. Auditions new talent. May specialize in in-house bookings and be designated according to establishment as Concert Manager.

For Additional Career Information Write

American Music Conference   request *Careers in Music*
1000 Skokie Boulevard
Wilmette, IL   60091

Music Educators National Conference
1902 Association Drive
Reston, VA   22091

PHYSICAL EDUCATION/ RECREATION MAJOR

With today's emphasis on physical fitness and life-long sports, a physical education major should examine the many

WITH YOUR CERTIFICATION, CONSIDER . . .

options in recreation, such as individual recreation, recreation for the aged, private recreation (camping facilities, health spas, industry), and public recreation (YMCA, teaching a specific sport). Also be sure to explore P.E. for the handicapped, junior college teaching, dance therapy, and the choices for "all majors" in Appendix I listing Federal Government jobs.

Investigate These Career Options

Recreation Leader

Conducts recreation activities with assigned groups in public department of voluntary agency. Organizes, promotes, and develops interest in activities. Cooperates with other staff members in conducting community wide events. Works with neighborhood groups to determine recreation interests and needs of all ages.

Camp Director

Directs the activities of a recreation or youth work camp. Plans programs of recreational and educational activities. Hires and supervises camp staff. May keep records regarding finances, personnel actions, enrollments, and program activities related to camp business operations and budget allotments.

Sales Representative, Recreation and Sporting Goods (Wholesale)

Sells amusement and sporting goods, such as hunting and fishing equipment, camping equipment, athletic equipment, playground equipment, and toys and games.

Hospital Recreation Director

Plans, organizes, and directs medically approved recreation program for patients in hospitals and other institutions. Directs and organizes such activities as adapted sports, dramatics, social activities, and arts and crafts. Regulates content of program in accordance with patients' abilities, needs, and interests. May prepare reports for a patient's physician or treatment team describing patient's reactions, and symptoms indicative of progress or regression.

Sports Announcer

Announces radio and/or television programs to audiences. May describe sporting events during game from direct observation or announce sports news received at station for radio or television broadcasting.

Manager, Hotel Recreational Facilities

Manages hotel or motel recreational facilities. Advises guests of available activities, such as swimming, skating, boating, and other sports. May process applications for rental of cabanas, docking of yachts, and membership. Hires and directs activities of subordinates. Compiles record of receipts collected for use of facilities.

Social Director

Plans and organizes recreational activities and creates friendly atmosphere for guests in hotels and resorts or for passengers on board ship. Greets new arrivals, introduces them to other guests, acquaints them with recreational facilities, and encourages them to participate in group activities. Ascertains interests of group and evaluates available equipment and facilities to plan activities.

For Additional Information Write

American Alliance for Health, Physical Education and Recreation
1900 Association Drive
Reston, VA 22091

WITH YOUR CERTIFICATION, CONSIDER . . .

National Recreation and Park Association
1601 North Kent Street
Arlington, VA   22209

Personnel Division
National Council of YMCA's
101 North Wacker Drive
Chicago, IL   60606

Boy Scouts of America
Personnel and Training Division
P.O. Box 61030
Dallas/Ft. Worth Airport Station
Dallas, TX   75261

American Association for Leisure and Recreation
1201 Sixteenth Street, N.W.
Washington, DC   20036

American Camping Association
Bradford Woods
Martinsville, IN   46151

National Industrial Recreational Association
20 North Wacker Drive
Chicago, IL   60606

PHYSICS MAJOR

Physics majors possess inquisitive minds, imagination, math ability, and a body of scientific knowledge. Physics teachers have acquired many administrative skills. Private industry is the largest employer of physics majors. Companies that manufacture chemicals, electrical equipment, aircraft, missiles, and medical instruments can use your skills for production, research, and technical sales and service. Certainly there are many other options; these are suggested as starting points. Be sure to check out the many Federal Government options listed in Appendix I.

Investigate These Career Options

Sales Representative, Dental and Medical Equipment and Supplies

Sells medical and dental equipment and supplies (except drugs and medicines) to doctors, dentists, hospitals, medical schools, and retail establishments. Studies data describing new products to develop sales approach. Compiles data on equipment and supplies preferred by customers. Advises customers about equipment for a given need based on technical knowledge of products.

Quality Control Technician

Tests and inspects products at various stages of production and compiles and evaluates statistical data to determine and maintain quality and reliability of products. Interprets engineering drawings, schematic diagrams, or formulas to arrive at specified quality and reliability standards. Selects products for tests at specified stages in production, and tests for things such as dimensions, performance, and mechanical, electrical, or chemical characteristics. May specialize in one area of quality control, such as design, incoming material, process control, product evaluation, inventory control, product reliability, research and development, or administrative application.

Technical Illustrator

Lays out and draws illustrations for reproduction in reference works, brochures, and technical manuals dealing with assembly, installation, operation, maintenance, and repair of machines, tools, and equipment. Prepares drawings from blueprints, de-

WITH YOUR CERTIFICATION, CONSIDER . . .

signs, mock-ups, and photoprints by methods and techniques suited to specified reproduction process.

Science Editor

Directs and coordinates activities of writers engaged in preparing technical, scientific, or other material for publication, such as in manuals, briefs, proposals, instruction books, catalogs, and related technical publications. Analyzes developments in specific field to determine need for revisions, corrections, and changes in previously published materials, and need for new materials. May specialize in particular type of publication.

Physicist

Conducts research into phases of physical phenomena, develops theories and laws on basis of observation and experiments, and devises methods to apply laws and theories of physics to industry, medicine, and other fields. Performs experiments with masers, lasers, cyclotrons, betatrons, telescopes, mass spectrometers, electron microscopes, and other equipment. Describes and expresses observations and conclusions in mathematical terms. Works under direction of supervisor or senior physicist.

Patent Examiner (Government Service)

Searches patent files to ascertain originality of patent application.

Food and Drug Inspector (Government Service)

Inspects establishment where foods, drugs, cosmetics, and similar consumer items are manufactured, handled, stored, or sold to enforce legal standards of sanitation, purity, and grading. Ascertains that required licenses and permits have been obtained and are displayed. Prepares reports on each establishment visited, including findings and recommendations for action. May test products, using variety of specialized test equipment, such as ultraviolet lights and filter guns.

ALTERNATIVE CAREERS FOR TEACHERS

For Additional Career Information Write

American Institute of Physics
335 East Forty-fifth Street
New York, NY 10017

Pharmaceutical Manufacturers Association
1155 Fifteenth Street, N.W.
Washington, DC 20005

Office of Personnel Management
1900 E Street, N.W.
Washington, DC 20415

Sales and Marketing Executives International
380 Lexington Avenue
New York, NY 10019

National Association of Science Writers
P.O. Box 294
Greenlawn, NY 11740

POLITICAL SCIENCE MAJOR

Your understanding of political institutions and political and administrative processes makes you well qualified for positions in and out of government. Political science involves needs assessment, data analysis, problem solving, consensus seeking, discussion and debate, and ultimately the skillful maintenance of order while creating change for the better. Knowledge of political processes and possession of such skills have broad application in a rapidly changing world. Trade associations, public interest groups, business firms, and the Federal Government would be interested in your skills. You should also think

WITH YOUR CERTIFICATION, CONSIDER . . .

about applying your analytical skills to marketing, management, public relations, personnel work, or finance.

Investigate These Career Options

Reporter

Collects and analyzes information about newsworthy events in order to write news story for publication or broadcast. Receives assignments or evaluates leads and news tips to develop story ideas. Gathers and verifies factual information regarding story through interview, observation, and research. Organizes material, determines slant or emphasis. May specialize in one type of reporting, such as political affairs.

Foreign Service Officer (Government Service)

Represents interests of United States Government and nationals by conducting relations with foreign nations and international organizations and by protecting and advancing political, economic, and commercial interests overseas. Renders personal service to Americans abroad and to foreign nationals traveling to the United States. May be designated according to the basic field of specialization, as Administrative Officer, Commercial Officer, Consular Officer, Cultural Affairs Officer, Diplomatic Officer, Economic Officer, Information Officer, Political Officer, or Public Affairs Officer.

Import/Export Agent

Coordinates activities of international traffic division of import/export agency and negotiates settlements between foreign and domestic shippers. May contact custom officials to effect release of incoming freight and resolve custom delays.

Pollster

Organizes and conducts public opinion surveys and interprets results. Analyzes and interprets results of studies, and prepares reports detailing findings, recommendations, or conclusions.

Lobbyist

Contacts and confers with members of legislature and other holders of public office to persuade them to support legislation favorable to client's interest. Studies proposed legislation to determine possible effects on interests of client, who may be a person, a specific group, or the general public. May contact regulatory agencies and testify at public hearings to enlist support for client's interests.

Intelligence Specialist (Government Service)

Evaluates data concerning subversive activities, enemy propaganda, and military or political conditions in foreign countries to facilitate counteraction by the United States.

For Additional Career Information Write

Board of Examiners
Foreign Service
Box 9317
Rosslyn Station
Arlington, VA 22209

American Political Science Association
1527 New Hampshire Avenue, N.W.
Washington, DC 20036

American Importers Association
11 West Forty-second Street
New York, NY 10036

WITH YOUR CERTIFICATION, CONSIDER . . .

Radio-Television News Directors Association
1735 DeSales Street, N.W.
Washington, DC 20036

PSYCHOLOGY MAJOR

The strength of your major is its diversity. The special insights and understandings you have of people open options for you in human service settings such as mental health centers, senior citizen centers, drug and alcohol abuse programs (especially in prevention and education), and hospitals. Your expertise is also needed in business and industry, research establishments, and government agencies.

Investigate These Career Options

Credit Manager

Directs and coordinates activities of workers engaged in conducting credit investigations and in collecting delinquent accounts of customers of commercial establishment, department store, or bank. Reviews and evaluates applications, substantiated data, and recommendations in order to determine credit validity. May also submit delinquent accounts to attorney or outside agency for collection.

Personnel Psychologist

Develops and applies psychological techniques to personnel administration, management, and marketing problems. Observes details of work and interviews workers and supervisors to establish physical, mental, educational, and other job requirements. May specialize in development and application of such techniques as job analysis and classification, personnel interviewing, ratings, and vocational tests for use in selection, placement, promotion, and training of workers.

Sales Agent, Psychological Tests and Industrial Relations

Sells programs of industrial relations, public relations, psychological counseling, and psychological, intelligence, and aptitude testing to schools and business organizations. Interviews management officials of business to explain advantages of utilizing services offered. Analyzes program needs of organization and recommends appropriate psychological or other testing program.

Probation Officer

Engages in activities related to probation of juvenile or adult offenders. Determines which juvenile cases fall within jurisdiction of the court and which should be adjusted informally or referred to other agencies. Conducts prehearing or presentence investigations of adults and juveniles by interviewing offender, family, and others concerned.

Community Relations Worker

Plans, organizes, and works with community groups concerned with social problems of community. Stimulates, promotes, and coordinates agencies, groups, and individuals to meet identified needs. Studies and assesses strengths and weaknesses of existing resources. Interprets needs, programs, and services to agencies, groups, and individuals involved and provides leadership and assistance.

Market Research Analyst

Researches market conditions in local, regional, or national area to determine potential sales of product or service. Establishes research methodology and designs format for data gathering,

WITH YOUR CERTIFICATION, CONSIDER . . .

such as survey, opinion poll, or questionnaire. Examines and analyzes statistical data to forecast future marketing trends.

Personnel Recruiter

Interviews job applicants to select persons meeting employer's qualifications. Reviews completed application and evaluates applicant's work history, education and training, job skills, salary desired, and physical and personal qualifications. Records additional skills, knowledge, abilities, interests, test results, and other data pertinent to classification, selection, and referral. May seek out potential applicants and try to interest them in applying for open positions.

For Additional Career Information Write

American Psychological
   Association
1200 Seventeenth Street, N.W.
Washington, DC 20036

have published a number of career pamphlets and books and publish an employment bulletin

National Council on Crime and Delinquency
411 Hackensack Avenue
Hackensack, NJ 07601

International Personnel Management Association
1850 K Street, N.W.
Suite 870
Washington, DC 20006

Sales and Marketing Executives International
380 Lexington Avenue
New York, NY 10017

ALTERNATIVE CAREERS FOR TEACHERS

SCHOOL COUNSELING MAJOR

A school counselor "wears many hats." You can translate those hats into skills: good listening skills, oral and written communication skills, effective facilitating, an ability to identify needs and develop solutions, mentoring, a talent for inspiring trust and confidence, an ability to develop effective interpersonal relationships, and administrative abilities. Your personal list will include many additional skills as you examine your responsibilities as a school counselor. These skills are transferable to many positions not bearing the title *counselor*. If you choose to continue counseling, remember that counselors work in a variety of settings. Colleges and universities, mental health agencies, rehabilitation agencies, correctional facilities, public employment agencies, and business and industry all employ counselors.

Investigate These Career Options

College Career Planning and Placement Counselor

Coordinates activities of job placement service for college students and graduates. Develops placement office procedures. Establishes workloads, assigns tasks, and reviews results. Conducts in-service training programs for placement personnel. Interviews applicants to determine qualifications and eligibility for employment. Assists individuals to develop employment plans based on appraisals of aptitudes, interests, and personality characteristics, and to plan curriculum accordingly. Contacts prospective employers to determine needs and to explain placement service. Arranges on-campus interviews between employers and graduating students to facilitate placement of graduates.

WITH YOUR CERTIFICATION, CONSIDER . . .

Sales Agent, Psychological Tests and Industrial Relations

Sells programs of industrial relations, public relations, psychological counseling, and psychological, intelligence, and aptitude testing to schools and business organizations. Analyzes program needs of organization and recommends appropriate psychological or testing program.

Admissions Evaluator/Counselor

Examines academic record of students to determine eligibility for graduation or for admission to college, university, or graduate school. Compares transcripts of courses with school entrance or degree requirements and prepares evaluation form listing courses needed for graduation. Studies course prerequisites, degree equivalents, and accreditation of schools, and computes grade point averages to establish students' qualifications for admission, transfer, or graduation.

Probation Officer

Engages in activities related to probation of juveniles or adult offenders. Determines which juvenile cases fall within jurisdiction of the court and which should be adjusted informally or referred to other agencies. Conducts prehearing or presentence investigations of adults and juveniles by interviewing offender, family, and others concerned.

Caseworker, Social Services

Counsels and aids individuals and families requiring assistance of social service agency. Interviews clients with problems, such as personal and family adjustments, finances, employment, and physical and mental impairments, to determine nature and degree of problem. Refers clients to community resources and other organizations. May be designated Caseworker, Child Welfare; Family Caseworker; Delinquency Prevention Caseworker.

ALTERNATIVE CAREERS FOR TEACHERS

Vocational Adviser/Counselor

Counsels individuals and provides group educational and vocational guidance services. Collects, organizes, and analyzes information about individuals through records, tests, interviews, and professional sources, to appraise their interests, aptitudes, abilities, and personal characteristics. Must take Civil Service Exam for employment positions with government service. May be designated according to area of activity, as Counselor, Veterans Administration (government service); Counselor, State Employment Division (government service); Counselor, Vocational Rehabilitation (government service).

Parole Officer

Engages in activities related to conditional release of juveniles or adult offenders from correctional institutions. Establishes relationship with offender and familiarizes self with offender's social history prior to and during institutionalization. Participates in formulation and development of release plan. Provides supervision of offenders upon release by conducting a plan of treatment and interviews. Employed by correctional institution or parole agency.

Personnel Recruiter

Interviews job applicants to select persons meeting employer's qualifications. Reviews completed application and evaluates applicant's work history, education and training, job skills, salary desired, and physical and personal qualifications. Records additional skills, knowledge, abilities, interests, test results, and other data pertinent to classification, selection, and referral. May engage in research or follow-up activities to evaluate selection and placement techniques.

WITH YOUR CERTIFICATION, CONSIDER . . .

For Additional Career Information Write

National Council on Crime and Delinquency
411 Hackensack Avenue
Hackensack, NJ   07601

American Personnel and Guidance Association
2 Skyline Place, Suite 400
5203 Leesburg Pike
Falls Church, VA   22041

College Placement Council, Inc.
62 Highland Avenue
Bethlehem, PA   18017

National Rehabilitation Counseling Association
1522 K Street, N.W.
Washington, DC   20005

American Society for Training and Development
P.O. Box 5307
Madison, WI   53705

SECRETARIAL SCIENCE MAJOR

Your thorough knowledge of office procedures and operations and the administrative skills you have acquired in teaching provide you with a strong background for a second career. Explore options in banking, insurance, large businesses (employee training positions), and companies that manufacture and sell office equipment.

ALTERNATIVE CAREERS FOR TEACHERS

Investigate These Career Options

Bookkeeper

Keeps complete set of records of financial transactions of establishment. Verifies and enters details of transactions in account and cash journals. Balances books and compiles reports to show statistics such as cash receipts and expenditures, accounts payable and receivable, profit and loss, and other items pertinent to the operation of a business.

Sales Representative, Office Machines

Sells office machines, such as typewriters and adding, calculating, and duplicating machines, to business establishments or educational institutions. May instruct employees or purchasers in use of machine. May rent or lease machines. May be designated according to type of machine sold, as Sales Representative, Typewriters; Sales Representative, Stenographic Machines.

Office Manager

Coordinates activities of clerical personnel in establishment or organization. Analyzes and organizes office operations and procedures, such as typing, bookkeeping, preparation of payroll, flow of correspondence, filing, requisition of supplies, and other clerical services. Evaluates office production, revises procedures, or devises new forms to improve efficiency of workflow. Plans office layouts and initiates cost reduction programs.

Instructor, Correspondence School

Plans course of study for students enrolled in correspondence courses to obtain high school, college, or other specialized subject area instruction. Reviews enrollment applications and oversees mailing of course materials to students. Corrects, grades, and comments on lesson assignments submitted by

WITH YOUR CERTIFICATION, CONSIDER . . .

students. Corresponds with students to answer questions pertaining to course.

Sales Representative, Education Courses

Solicits applications for enrollment in technical, commercial, and industrial schools. Contacts prospects, explains courses offered by school, and quotes fees. Advises prospective students on selection of courses based on their education and vocational objectives. Compiles registration information. May be designated according to the specific type of school, as Sales Representative, Business Courses.

Training Representative

Prepares and conducts training program for employees of industrial, commercial, service, or governmental establishment. Confers with management to analyze work situation requiring preventive or remedial training for employees. Formulates teaching outline, selects or develops teaching aids, and conducts general or specialized training sessions.

Personnel Recruiter

Interviews job applicants to select persons meeting employer's qualifications. Reviews completed application and evaluates applicant's work history, education and training, job skills, salary desired, and physical and personal qualifications. Records additional skills, knowledge, abilities, interests, test results, and other data pertinent to classification, selection, and referral.

For Additional Career Information Write

American Society for Training and Development
P.O. Box 5307
Madison, WI   53705

ALTERNATIVE CAREERS FOR TEACHERS

National Secretaries Association
Suite G10, Crown Center
2440 Pershing Road
Kansas City, MO 64108

SOCIOLOGY MAJOR

Your major in sociology and experience in education provide you with a more than suitable background for other "people" positions. Employ your research skills to determine opportunities that exist for you. Youth work, social service agencies, law enforcement, state and Federal Government positions, and research organizations would be good starting places.

Investigate These Career Options

Pollster

Consults with government officials, civic bodies, research agencies, and political parties. Analyzes and interprets results of studies and prepared reports detailing findings, recommendations, or conclusions. May organize and conduct public opinion surveys and interpret results.

State Police Officer

Patrols state highways within assigned areas to enforce motor vehicle and criminal laws. Arrests or warns persons guilty of violating motor vehicle regulations and safe driving practices. Provides road information and assistance to motorists. Directs activities in accident or disaster area.

WITH YOUR CERTIFICATION, CONSIDER . . .

Public Relations Representative

Plans and conducts public relations program designed to create and maintain favorable public image for employer or client. Arranges for public relations efforts in order to meet needs, objectives, and policies of an individual, special interest group, business concern, nonprofit organization, or governmental agency, serving as in-house staff member or as outside consultant. Prepares and distributes fact sheets, news releases, or photographs to media representatives and other persons who may be interested in learning about or publicizing employer's activities or message.

Market Research Analyst

Researches market conditions in local, regional, or national area to determine potential sales of product or service. Gathers data on competitors and analyzes prices, sales, and methods of marketing and distribution. Collects data on customer preferences and buying habits.

Interviewer

Interviews applicants for television game shows and coordinates activities of contestants. Provides information to applicants concerning show's objective and format, and screens applicants for compliance with needs of show and established rules.

Caseworker, Child Welfare

Aids parents with child rearing problems and children and youth with difficulties in social adjustments. Investigates home conditions to protect children from harmful environment. Refers child and parent to appropriate community resources. Determines suitability of foster home and adoptive applicants.

ALTERNATIVE CAREERS FOR TEACHERS

Personnel Recruiter

Interviews job applicants to select persons meeting employer's qualifications. Reviews completed application and evaluates applicant's work history, education and training, job skills, salary desired, and physical and personal qualifications. Records additional skills, knowledge, abilities, interests, test results, and other data pertinent to classification, selection, and referral. May engage in research or follow-up activities to evaluate selection and placement techniques.

For Additional Career Information Write

American Sociological Association
Career and Research Division
1722 N Street, N.W.
Washington, DC 20036

Career Information
Public Relations Society of America, Inc.
845 Third Avenue
New York, NY 10022

National Council on
  Crime and Delinquency
411 Hackensack Avenue
Hackensack, NJ 07601

request *Careers in the Criminal Justice System*: *Police, Courts, Probation, Institutional Training and Treatment, Parole, Aftercare*

American Correctional Association
4321 Hartwick Road,
Suite L-208
College Park, MD 20740

6.

OCCUPATIONAL RESEARCH

Use a variety of resources to find your ideal career. The goal of this research is twofold: (1) to identify new career options that offer what you seek, and (2) to provide you with important occupational information for use in writing your resume and in target marketing (job seeking).

Begin your search with background reading to obtain an overview of the employment world. Develop a broad list of options. Then narrow the field. Permit your interests to guide further reading. Finally, conduct original research into viable options within your geographic area.

SOURCES OF GENERAL OCCUPATIONAL INFORMATION— BACKGROUND READING

Chapter 5 provides information about career options and lists sources of more specific information. The options listed are a sample of the many that exist for teachers. They are arranged according to teacher's educational background and reflect the data/people work level and readily transferable skills of teachers.

The Occupational Outlook Handbook, published biennially by the U.S. Department of Labor's Bureau of Labor Statistics, offers an overview of the world of work and contains summary information about several hundred occupations. Included are descriptions of the work, working conditions, places of employment, training or educational requirements, methods of entry, employment outlook, wages and benefit information, related occupations, and sources of additional information. An evening or two spent scanning this publication will be most informative.

Read critically and don't be totally put off by a dismal forecast in an area of interest to you. Remember that forecasting, even with the help of modern technology and the best of data, can be difficult. Consider your weatherman! A poor outlook merely means that you will face more competition for openings that do exist.

The Encyclopedia of Career and Vocational Guidance, Volume II (J.G. Ferguson Co., Illinois) gives information on major occupational groupings and covers specific career occupations. It is very similar to *The Occupational Outlook Handbook*.

The Occupational Outlook for College Graduates (U.S. Department of Labor; Bureau of Labor Statistics) is a guide to a broad range of occupations for which a college degree is, or is becoming, the usual background for employment. It also summarizes expected changes in the economy and provides analysis of the overall supply and demand situation for college graduates.

The College Placement Annual (The College Placement Council, Inc., P.O. Box 2263, Bethlehem, PA 80001) includes occupational needs anticipated by approximately one thousand corporate and government employers who normally recruit college graduates. It also indexes these employers both by occupation and by geographic area. This publication is usually available in public libraries and college placement offices.

The Occupational Outlook Quarterly (U.S. Department of Labor, Bureau of Labor Statistics) is a supplement to the larger volume and is available in the magazine section of the library. Published four times a year, it includes occupational forecasts and articles on a host of related topics: emerging opportunities for women, average incomes contrasted with income ranges, mid-life career change, careers within developing fields, and more. The articles provide references to additional resources. We suggest browsing through the recent issues.

Other general resources for occupational information can be found in a nearby high school's guidance office or the school media center. Most high schools have established a vertical file for occupational information and have collected assorted pamphlets, printouts, and leaflets about a wide variety of careers. Some publishers have made it their business to provide schools with well organized and readable occupational information, and some market complete filing systems. Check with the school counselor or librarian to see what resources are available.

OTHER TOOLS TO BROADEN OPTIONS AND GATHER BACKGROUND INFORMATION

Many interest inventories and occupational information systems have been devised which are useful in broadening one's options. They work by linking personal preferences to career options through a system which processes data both about yourself and about occupations. Since these systems sort data for you, they can also cloud the decision-making process. Use care to become informed about the options they suggest.

Many occupational information systems have been computerized and offer both search strategies and up-to-date career information. For instance, the Guidance Information System (GIS), published by Time Share Corporation, uses a national data base for its occupational file. Some states have developed their own systems.

ALTERNATIVE CAREERS FOR TEACHERS

In using computerized systems, you can input data about yourself and, after the computer has sorted it, retrieve a list of occupations linked to your input data. Changing the input changes the output, or list of options. Using a computer this way enables you to sift quickly through a large volume of information and to discover career options you may otherwise overlook. Given a variety of job titles, you can then request detailed descriptions of those which interest you and be guided to sources of more information. Since the occupational information in these computerized systems can be changed and updated easily, it tends to be quite current. The guidance office of your local high school, community college, or public library may provide access to an occupational information system.

As you analyze information from your reading and research, a broadened list of career options will begin to emerge. List them under the following categories:

1. The following job titles interest me:

   _____ _____
   _____ _____

2. These job titles might interest me but I need to obtain more information on them:

   _____ _____
   _____ _____

3. I would like to research these companies or areas of work to determine which job titles are used which might be of interest to me:

   _____ _____
   _____ _____

Any of the references listed under Sources of Occupational Information can assist you in obtaining more data about job titles of interest to you. You may find it helpful to develop a worksheet, similar to the one shown below, to record the facts you obtain.

OCCUPATIONAL RESEARCH

JOB RESEARCH SHEET

Job Title _____
Brief summary of the tasks performed in this job: _____
_____

Requirements: The following skills, abilities, knowledge and/or certificates are needed to perform this job: _____
_____

Qualifications: I have the following skills, abilities, knowledge and/or certificates relevant to this job: _____
_____

Salary range: _____
Job outlook (projected openings): _____
Career ladder (what options exist beyond the entry position):
_____

List organizations or employers that might hire someone to do this job: _____
_____

Resources to obtain more information: _____
_____

Names of people I might contact to find out more about this job title: _____
_____

Record below any additional information or your interest level for this job title: _____
_____

Recording this information on specific job titles will provide you with an orderly means of retrieving the data for future analysis and evaluation. Should the position now be of even greater interest, this information will form a good foundation for the additional knowledge you will acquire as you begin networking and subsequently interviewing for information.

SOURCES FOR ORIGINAL RESEARCH — NETWORKING

All published occupational information comes originally from the person doing a job or the person paying to have the job done. Since much occupational information is dated by the time it is printed, your own original research will provide the most up-to-date information. So then, once you have a sense of direction from your library research, you also need to do some original research.

Networking is the most effective way to conduct your original research and offers many other benefits. Networking is the establishment of personal contacts to create a web-like communication system. The network acts as a referral system providing you with contacts who can furnish you with information in a wide range of areas associated with a career search. For instance, you can obtain information on job titles, specific companies, positions within those companies, actual or anticipated openings, additional people to contact, suggestions for improving your resume, feedback on interviews, and more.

Who's in your network? You have many more contacts than you would imagine. Begin now to jot down the names of all the people you know fairly well or who know you fairly well, regardless of whether you've seen them in the past year or not. We'd expect that you would be able to compile a list of at least fifty to sixty people with considerable ease. Here are a few suggestions for people to include:

- friends (look at your Christmas card list)

- relatives and their close friends

- neighbors (current and past)

- fellow club members

OCCUPATIONAL RESEARCH

- members of your church (don't forget the pastor, priest, or rabbi)

- your classmates (at any school or college you attended)

- parents of your students

- teachers of your children

- parents of your children's peers

- co-workers and former co-workers

Don't forget community contacts such as your doctor, dentist, veterinarian, lawyer, insurance agent, real estate agent, druggist, beautician/barber, or banker.

The next step is to determine what information you need and which of these people might have the information OR be able to lead you to those who do. Networking works best when you have a clear goal in mind. You must tell people specifically what it is you need and at the same time use the moment to teach them a little about yourself. Don't say, "I'm looking for a job. Do you know of any openings?" Instead, you might say, "I'm a journalism major with extensive experience in publications. Do you know of any individuals working in public relations with whom I could speak to get more insights into the profession?"

If you state clearly what information you are seeking and do not put people on the spot by asking them to recommend you for a job, you will find many, many people willing to help you. While it is not unusual for this process to lead you to job openings and interviews, you will find people more receptive if you are seeking only information.

Frequently this concept of networking is uncomfortable for teachers. Educators for the most part are accustomed to being in charge, being the ones who are asked to help others. When they have to seek help from others, some feel it makes them look weak. Asking for help — in this case information — is certainly

ALTERNATIVE CAREERS FOR TEACHERS

not a sign of weakness.

Another aspect of networking that often serves as an obstacle or blockage for teachers is their perception that networking is USING people. If you never intend to repay the favor, then perhaps it could be viewed as a brassy technique. The concept of networking is that at some point you will be called upon to assist someone else, and, when you do so you repay those who have previously helped you. Obviously, you may never be able to help the person who assisted you, but you can help someone.

We contacted ex-teachers, personnel managers, and placement advisers for their insights and suggestions about making the career change from teaching. In each case, if the person we contacted couldn't help, we were referred to someone who could. People were very willing to speak with us and to aid us. You too can expect your own research into alternative career opportunities to be a reassuring and interesting process. Most people do enjoy and take pride in their work, and they don't mind talking about it. Talking to people, by the way, was the suggestion most frequently offered by those we contacted. The usefulness of networking techniques is evident from the statements below:

> I made a decision to plug into my networking system on the very day I was pink slipped. I announced in every one of my high school classes that I was being laid-off and that I was looking for a job in sales. If anyone had any leads for openings, I'd appreciate knowing about them.
>
> The next day a student came up to me after class and said that she had talked with her father and that he'd like to meet with me. The interview the following week led to a full-time position in sales for a major soft drink company. After one year in that job, I became a sales rep for a Fortune 500 company selling medical supplies. I am now completing my second year with this company. Our district won the top sales award nationally and none of us had more than two years with the company. My wife and I just returned from a fully paid trip to Hawaii. I'm so glad I asked my students for their help!
>
> Fortune 500 Sales Rep

OCCUPATIONAL RESEARCH

Networking is a very effective strategy in obtaining a new career. Teachers looking for new careers need to meet as many people as they can who can provide vital information about a field of interest and who can help lead ultimately to a desirable job. People generally get jobs through other people. The demand is there, but you have to look for it.

Career Counselor

I'd advise teachers to research the market, to become familiar with companies they like. Talking to people about an organization helps to clarify what you can do within and for the company.

Personnel Manager for a large metropolitan utility

It has been two years since I left teaching and as I think back on making that move, I'm reminded that lots of very nice people offered me encouragement. I'd suggest that a teacher wanting to change careers get out and talk to people outside of education. They will find understanding people who are willing to advise and to help.

Ex-teacher now working for a major insurance company

Tips on Networking

- Don't be afraid to use your network. It is your greatest outside resource.

- Give as much as you get. The old saying "you reap what you sow" applies here. People accustomed to using networking overwhelmingly agree that helping others helps them.

- Follow-up on leads received through networking. If people are going to take the time to contact acquaintances on your behalf, it can be quite irritating to later be told, "I thought you said _____ was going to call. I've never heard from him/her." People will not be so willing to help in the future.

- Do report back to anyone who gives you a lead. People like to be helpful and appreciate knowing if the lead was a help to you. It is also a great time to repeat your thanks.

- Do not pass up any opportunities to network. You never know where you will find that golden lead; it could be tonight's social activity.

- Don't expect your network to function strictly as a job placement service. Don't put everyone you know on the spot by asking them to recommend you for a job.

- Don't be discouraged if someone seems unwilling to help. Keep your thoughts on all of the helpful contacts you have had.

Start some networking. Put out feelers. Make contacts. Utilize the referrals that result, and request more leads from them. Advertise by word of mouth. Initiate conversations and let people know what it is you are looking for. As you do so, keep in mind the job search of a liberal arts graduate and this statement that an Assistant Dean of a university career planning and placement department shared with us:

> Liberal Arts graduates tend to get their jobs by their own initiative. They have a longer average transition period from school to work than do graduates in more technical and scientific fields. Longitudinal studies, over ten to fifteen years, however, show that they have met with many career successes. There *are* good opportunities which are not widely published; most of these jobs are filled by referral or through personal initiative.
>
> For teachers, too, there is no natural marketplace. The possibilities and combinations of employable skills and talents are almost limitless; they depend on the individual's profile and interests. Ex-teachers have some advantages over liberal arts graduates in the areas of leadership, experience, and self-assurance. The opportunities are there. They need only to be sought out.

OCCUPATIONAL RESEARCH

NETWORKING LEADS TO INFORMATIONAL INTERVIEWS

Once you identify the people who can provide you with the insights and information you desire, try to arrange a short, informal, face-to-face meeting with them. Such a meeting is referred to as an informational interview. Depending on how well you know the person, you can arrange the meeting by either letter or phone.

Before the interview, develop a list of questions you would like to discuss. Your unique situation and reasons for contacting this person will provide you with many of the topics. You may want to gather information about a specific job title, labor market conditions, potential employers, trends in the field. You could request advice on the direction to follow in your job search and get reactions/evaluations to your qualifications and resume (if you've developed one). Always try to obtain the names of others in the field to continue expanding your network.

Frequently asked questions are:

- What do you like about your job?

- What are the things you would change?

- What are the major problems or challenges facing someone in this position?

- How do you spend your day? (tasks, etc.)

- How does one gain entry into this field?

- What options exist beyond the initial job?

- What are the three most important qualities necessary for success in this position?

- What associations do people in this field belong to?

- Which other companies also hire people in this capacity?

- What else should I be asking you?

- Do you know of another person in a position similar to yours but with a different firm who I might talk with?

   A couple words of caution are in order here. Be considerate of the amount of time you take from the individual. One half hour should be sufficient, and, by all means, maximum should be one hour. Also remember to evaluate the information you get from the individual. Everyone is unique and what one person may dislike in a position, another may thrive on. Despite the fact that a person employed in a particular position "says it is so," you still need to evaluate that information in relation to your own skills, abilities, likes, dislikes, and personality. Try to obtain more than one person's view of a career. Consider the varied responses one might get in having information interviews with teachers regarding the field of education. One view alone is unlikely to present an accurate picture.

Tips on Interviewing for Information

- Be prepared for the meeting. Refrain from asking questions that are obvious from basic reading. You might want to share some information you have acquired about the position and test the validity of the data.

OCCUPATIONAL RESEARCH

- Do follow up each informational interview with a short thank you note.

- Keep phone calls short and limited to business matters. Again, be considerate of the amount of time you request of others.

- Don't express dissatisfaction/disillusionment in the informational interviews or that "you really aren't sure you want to leave teaching." This makes people very hesitant about giving you leads.

- Don't put the person in the role of a personal friend and confide that you perceive your experiences or skills to be limited.

- Keep a card file of your interviews. A form is suggested in Chapter 7 that can be adapted for this purpose.

Networking and interviewing for information take a lot of time. You will also find them to be fun, exhilarating, and packed full of new knowledge. They are active processes as opposed to passive ones. They are a way of *making* things happen rather than letting things happen. Both are concepts taught by professional career training firms and both are quite successful.

You are on your way. Having a sense of direction, and knowing where you want to go, is preparation for your next endeavor — getting there. If you established your network and organized the research about yourself and about interesting career options, then you have already taken some giant steps. You now need merely to get that information to the person or persons who can give you the job you seek. We offer this motto for success in your next endeavor, marketing:

> Early to bed and early to rise;
> Get to work and advertise!

7.
RESUMES

A good resume is an advertisement. Like any advertisement, your resume must convince the buyer that your product is worth additional investigation — an interview.

To advertise effectively, you must first have a well-conceived product and identify parties who would be interested in it. An effective resume means you define your product's capabilities — your skills, accomplishments, and expertise. It also means identifying organizations in need of this product. If you have not begun this sorting and self-analysis, drafting a resume may be helpful. It can clarify things. To compose a resume without focusing both on your skills and your career target is like taking a shot in the dark. You're likely to miss by a mile.

A controversy exists today over the merits of the resume. In the past, in better economic climates, the resume was a valuable tool for obtaining an interview. Today hundreds of resumes are received for every advertised job opening. Time does not permit management to read every resume. In many instances, secretaries will discard those resumes that do not meet certain qualifications. The resumes that make it to the inner office may again be cursorily evaluated to narrow the interview group to a manageable size. If you are seeking jobs in an advertised market, be prepared to compose a powerful advertisement via your resume.

Career opportunities in the hidden job market do not rely as heavily on a written resume. Therefore, the importance of writing a resume is not so great. The hidden job market consists of the thousands of openings which are never advertised or made known to the general public. At any given time, more job openings exist in the hidden job market than in the advertised one.

RESUMES

Your networking and informational interviews will become your source of knowledge for openings in the hidden market.

In our experience of assisting teachers with career change and in conducting career change workshops, we have come to the conclusion that there is tremendous value in preparing a resume, especially a functional resume, even if you have little intention of using it. It is an opportunity to gain heightened awareness by taking your background and putting it in the foreground. It is a task, no matter how laborious, that you should take charge of yourself. Do not delegate it to someone else. Once you complete a beginning draft, then share it with others for their reactions and evaluations. The remainder of this chapter will assist you in completing that first draft.

WHICH RESUME — TRADITIONAL OR FUNCTIONAL?

The two most used types of resumes are the traditional (also known as the chronological) resume and the functional resume. The emphasis in the traditional or chronological resume is on past employment experience and education. It is the easiest type of resume to write, most widely used, and most familiar to those receiving it. It is the best form for a teacher seeking a position within education. However, it is not the best form for a teacher desiring to move out of education. This form of resume can "scream teacher" and does nothing to assist the reader in transferring your valuable skills to the business setting.

Our "scream teacher" comment often causes some raised eyebrows among educators. They are proud of being teachers and rightfully so. However, equally true is the fact that as professionals we have not done a very good job of teaching the general public that our skills are quite transferable. Often teachers themselves are skeptical; they view their experience as limited and reflect that view in the query, "What else can I do but teach?" While you will find many people in companies, especially those with positions in sales, most receptive to hiring teachers, you are also going to find many who you will have to "teach" or sell the idea of the transferability of your assets. To be successful, you need to understand your skills and their application to business so that you convey that same confidence and pride as you talk to prospective employers. The experience of writing a resume will help you see your skills in a new light and prepare you to market them in new settings.

The second type of resume, the functional resume, stresses skills. It capitalizes on the skills and abilities that you possess and desire to transfer to a new area of employment. Teachers find it a far more effective way to advertise. Although it is not the most conventional form, the functional resume is gaining acceptance. There is still, however, a slight risk that the uninitiated screener will withhold it from the inner office.

Samples of a traditional (chronological) and functional resumes are included later in this chapter. There is no exact form that either style of resume must follow. Your knowledge of your own unique abilities and the demands of the job will determine what qualities or information you will need to stress.

Beware of fad resumes that are less recognizable than familiar forms. While the intent is to make them stand apart from the other hundred or so, they seldom work. Remember, if you choose to use a resume, its purpose is to get you an interview. If it isn't accomplishing that, reevaluate it. Share it with friends in business and ask for suggestions.

WRITING RESUME STATEMENTS

If you elect to use a functional resume, you will write statements that accentuate your professional experiences and accomplishments. We will refer to these statements as resume statements. Scan the examples of functional resumes in this chapter. Read the statements listed under the headings Professional Experiences or Accomplishments. What are you thinking as you read them? Are you saying, "Gee, I've never done anything like that in all my years of teaching!" If so, take heart, because we believe most teachers have numerous professional accomplishments requiring superior skill and ability; they just need assistance in using their creativity to view those skills and experience in a broadened perspective, and to translate them into language that is meaningful to the business setting.

Let's analyze one common skill area. Teachers are experienced public speakers. You make presentations to your students and confer with parents during parent conferences and open houses. Many of you have spoken to PTA groups at one time or another and made presentations for your peers in department, building, or district meetings. Some may even have presented innovative ideas or discussed topics of common concern at schools in surrounding areas, at association or professional meetings, or at educational conferences on a local, state, or national level. These platform or stand-up speaking skills can be emphasized even though we know they are an integral part of being an educator. The topic you spoke on is probably of little importance. What is important is that you can document experience as a public speaker. Here are some ways to phrase that professional experience.

- Experienced public speaker. Made presentations daily to groups of thirty.

- Presented seminars on local, state, and national level on a variety of topics.

- Extensive platform experience (highlight here your specific experience)

- Speaker skilled at preparing content material and visual aids, at introducing new concepts to large and small groups, at reading audience reaction, and responding to achieve understanding.

- Directed the goal-oriented work activities for groups of twenty-five, prepared and delivered explanations and instructions on a daily (or hourly) basis.

When writing your resume statements, use action words to maximize each skill or accomplishment and make it come to life. This is something which seems very difficult for teachers to do. Granted, you do not want to say you have done something that you have not, but neither should you underrate experiences or say such things as:

"I talked to the PTA about summer reading with students when the regularly scheduled speaker didn't show. My state seminar was for an educational conference that was hosted by our school and everyone on staff was urged to participate. That national conference was a meeting hosted in our city; my principal approached me at the last minute because he was program chairman and was desperate for some additional seminar choices.

Teachers tend not to view their skills as very special; they take these abilities for granted. As they begin the task of describing their uniqueness in action words they sometimes become uncomfortable and frequently comment, "This is a lot of *&*#&¢!" Is it? Certainly not! Do you or do you not possess these skills and have these experiences? If you don't effectively advertise yourself — or toot your own horn — no one else will. Be proud of the things you do well. It is a mistake to think that everyone else can do them too. Ask yourself this: If a salesman started in a new territory that had ten accounts and within six months added twenty new accounts, would he say that he added twenty new accounts in six months? Rather, he would say he increased the number of accounts in his territory by two hundred percent within the first six months. A matter of semantics, certainly, but the fact remains that he did what he said. Don't take *your* skills for granted. Express them this positively.

Suppose the position you are seeking requires a strong written communication skill. What from your teaching experience can you use to document this skill? Have you written any units, any articles for the school newsletter or local newspaper,

RESUMES

scripts for school programs, grant applications, research projects, or any in-depth evaluations? Make a list of all the ways you have used your writing skills in teaching. List, too, all of the things you have written. Analyze this list and then write a resume statement which will document the strength of your writing. Remember, effective writing and public speaking are two of the most sought after and marketable skills in business. They are also skills few people possess or can document to the degree that teachers can. Capitalize on that!

The following are additional suggestions for more practice in writing resume statements:

(1) Sometimes it seems easier to write resume statements for someone else rather than ourselves. Using the sample chronological resume in this chapter, rework it into a functional resume. Draw on the experiences this job seeker has listed and imagine the additional tasks he performed plus the skills necessary to perform them and write new resume statements with his stated job objective in mind.

(2) Think of someone in teaching with whom you are well acquainted. Write some resume statements which apply to that person, documenting a variety of their skills.

(3) Invite three or four teachers to a brainstorm session where you will all work together to practice writing resume statements. Take a particular skill (oral or written communication, organizing, motivating, program planning, supervising, problem solving, etc.) and use the experience of one participant on which to base the statement. Write the resume statement, then rewrite it making it even stronger, more dynamic.

(4) Play *Top That* with a few other teachers who are also struggling with writing resume statements. Decide on one skill that you wish to work on and have every one in the group write down all the experience they have had related to that skill (see suggestions in number three). Select one of these sheets for use by the group. Then, the first player makes a general statement about the skill and passes the paper to the next player. That player

must expand upon the first statement (using information from the paper) and TOP the previous statement. Continue in this manner until you cannot TOP THAT and still keep the statement true. In all likelihood, the final sentence will be an excellent example of a dynamic resume statement.

As you become more adept at writing resume statements, we hope you will also experience a change in attitude. Putting these skills on paper, making them sound as special as they are, and bridging them to the business setting is going to make them come to life and give you renewed confidence in your marketability. This confidence is essential to your success and is one of the foremost reasons we advised earlier that you develop a resume even if you have little intention of using it.

Most functional resumes contain five to eight resume statements depending on the layout of the copy, the experiences and skills of the person, and the job objective. All of your resume statements should document a skill required for the position you are seeking. If your volunteer work is not relevant to the job for which you are creating the resume, then don't include it. Selling newspapers in the middle of a busy intersection is not something that will be of interest to the employer looking for a quality control technician, though it may be something you would wish to include if applying for a sales position or a position of high risk such as a stuntman.

As you compose your resume you will find that several of your statements will be more dynamic than others. Be sure to place these strategically. Your strongest statement or the one most applicable to the job should be placed first. Other strategic places to put strong statements are as second and as last. A person receiving your resume generally reads the first statement; if that captures his/her interest he/she will usually read the second or will often drop to the last one. Rare is the reader who reads each statement sequentially while scanning several hundred resumes with the task of eliminating them. Even if you were fortunate enough to get a person who does read every line, you would still want to start out strong and, of course, end up with a strong last statement. Arrange the remaining statements in any order that avoids repetition in the beginning action words.

If you are not planning a career change in the immediate future and have a time span to make the transition, give some thought to your present resume and, if needed, seek opportunities to strengthen it by adding experiences. Most educational associations have state and national conferences and many of these associations survey their membership and actively seek members willing to present one hour seminars at their conference. Surely you could present one of those units that you have developed and which worked out so well, or share insights you have gained from sponsoring a successful extracurricular activity. How about presenting your school's community service project or ways you motivated students in the recent fundraiser? In most of these seminar sessions you need not be an authority on a topic. Those who attend are more interested in what worked for you in hopes that it will assist them. And, speaking of associations — most we know of nearly beg people to get involved and run for office. Think of the resume potential — a chance to document leadership, administrative skills, motivating (increase the membership), etc. You need not even seek opportunities in a large organization. Analyze your own building and district for the potential. There are opportunities, you need only take advantage of them.

FINISHING THE FIRST DRAFT

Writing resume statements is the hardest part of completing this first draft. The rest is quite simple in comparison. The next step is to decide if you wish to include a job objective on your resume. Give thought to this matter. It is a practice that is currently quite accepted but which can also have limitations.

A job objective describes the position you are seeking. It is placed near the top of the resume directly under your name and other identifying data. The remainder of the resume then shows the reader the expertise and experience you bring to the employer for that position. The job objective is stated in no more than two or three sentences and should not be so vague that it seems to encompass all known positions, but neither can it be too specific if you are planning to have only one resume.

Many of you will conduct several job searches simultaneously. One of the reasons for this is that the skills you really wish to use are applicable to more than one job title. If this is your situation, and you elect to include a job objective, you definitely have to develop more than one resume. In many instances, the resumes will be quite similar. The differences, of course, will be in the job objective and can also be seen in the ordering of your resume statements. While many of the statements will be the same, a few will appear on one resume which do not appear on the others. The job objective and the skills needed dictate which to use.

Another factor to consider is how general or specific to make the job objective. Do you say you are seeking a position in sales or do you say you desire a position as a specialized kind of sales representative (pharmaceutical, for example)? While the general objective of sales seems more practical, you need to put yourself in the position of the individual seeking to hire a pharmaceutical salesperson. Would you then be inclined to look more favorably on a candidate whose resume indicates he is looking for any sales job or on the person who is specifically seeking employment in the position you wish to fill? There is no absolute answer for this question. Each person will have to make a decision that they feel comfortable with and then field test the resume to see if it produces the desired outcome — interviews.

People frequently ask our preference regarding job objectives. We prefer the use of the more specific objective, even though this requires the individual to have as many resumes as positions they are seeking. We believe this extra effort pays off. However, we also know several people who have elected to use the broader objective who have been successful.

Another decision you will need to make as you complete your first draft concerns the layout of the resume. A good way to do this is to look at many sample resumes. Either select one that appeals to you or take the best parts of several resumes and combine them into a form that has eye appeal, is readable, and represents you well.

Tips for Preparing the Final Copy

- Your final copy should be no more than two pages long. One page is preferable.

- Make it neat, clear, and easy to read. The final copy should have no strikeovers or mispelled words.

- Be concerned about the layout of the resume. Do the parts you want emphasized stand out to the reader? The layout of the resume can highlight areas you wish to emphasize.

- Omit anything that will not validate your potential to do the job you seek.

- Do not give marital status, siblings, religion, national origin, or birthdate. These particulars do not contribute to your ability to perform the job and, in some cases, could cause you not to get an interview.

- Do not give height or weight unless they are known requirements for the job.

- Do not list hobbies or outside interests unless they have direct relevance to the position.

- Consider whether you want to include a job objective on your resume. This may be something that you can handle equally as effectively in a cover letter. The exception, of course, is if you are conducting only one job search and know the exact title of the job you are seeking. Even then, be aware that different companies attach different titles to the same job.

- Always keep the needs of the prospective employer in mind. Clearly and concisely project why you would be an asset in that position. Put the emphasis on what you offer, not what you want.

ALTERNATIVE CAREERS FOR TEACHERS

- Do not list salary desired.

- Do not list references.

- Don't rush the final copy. Developing a good resume takes time and several revisions.

When do you prepare this final copy? You should begin almost immediately to practice highlighting your skills by writing your resume statements. However, don't prepare a final draft and run to the printer too soon. You need to know exactly where you are going — what job you desire — so that every skill, ability, and accomplishment listed demonstrates your potential to be successful in that position.

Individuals who are simultaneously looking into several different kinds of jobs, and who choose to state a very specific job objective for each one usually do not have the resume typeset and printed. Instead they tailor the resume to the position, type it, and have access to *excellent* copy machines in which they can insert a high quality stock of paper and make several copies. Many teachers have access to media specialists and workrooms which are tremendous assets in producing a professional looking product.

Some teachers feel a great urgency to complete their resumes. They believe they should carry copies of it with them when they are interviewing for information. This isn't necessary, especially at first. If the person who is interviewing you is impressed enough to ask for a resume, simply reply, "I didn't bring one today, but I'd be delighted to stop back tomorrow and leave one." If you have been working on the resume all along, as suggested, you will know from the interview exactly which of your skills would be beneficial to this employer. Therefore, all you need to do is type a tailored copy and deliver it the following day. If you are not asked for a resume, chances are the interviewer really doesn't want a copy anyway.

When you believe you know exactly where you want to go — the job you are seeking and the skills and abilities you can market into it — then complete the final copy.

RESUMES

(Example of a Chronological Resume)

NORMAN REESE
26733 South River Road
Mt. Clemens, MI 48045
Telephone (313) 000-0000

OCCUPATIONAL GOAL: Wholesale Sales Representative for major pharmaceutical company

EDUCATION: Eastern Michigan University, Ypsilanti, Michigan 1969
    Master's Degree in Educational Leadership

Marshall University, Huntington, West Virginia 1964
    Bachelor of Arts Degree in Education
      Major: Chemistry
      Minor: Business Administration

EMPLOYMENT HISTORY:

Sept. 1979 to June, 1984 — <u>Student Affairs Coordinator</u>, Warwood High School, Mt. Clemens, Michigan

Assumed responsibility for designing, implementing and marketing a student activities program in a school that had 1200 students and 8 active clubs. Organized and supervised fund raiser that netted $10,000 in a single day for the student affairs program. Conducted needs assessment and evaluation of program. Program has grown substantially and is considered a "model" program by State Department of Education.

Sept. 1972 to June, 1979 — <u>Student Affairs Coordinator</u>, Pauli High School, Pauli, Michigan

Assumed full responsibility for operation of existing student activities program for 900 students. Program began with 10 active clubs, grew to 30 clubs by 1978 with 80% of student population participating and 90% of the faculty. Developed enrichment facet to the program by instituting after-school mini-seminars on topics of interest. Assigned administrative responsibilities in principal's absence. Speaker on successful student activities program at state level educational conferences.

Sept. 1964 to June, 1972 — <u>Chemistry Instructor</u>, Hughes High School, Bradberry, Michigan

Began teaching introductory chemistry classes, progressed to department chairperson. Designed and implemented advanced courses in chemistry. Fifteen percent of high school students completing these classes have elementary college chemistry courses waived. Judge on regional level for National Science Fair. Served on county committee to write substance abuse program for high school students.

REFERENCES: Available on request

ALTERNATIVE CAREERS FOR TEACHERS

(Example of a Functional Resume)

MARILYN DEGRIECK
24917 Star Valley   St. Clair Shores, MI 48080
Telephone (313) 000-0000

JOB OBJECTIVE

A management position in employee retraining, employee upgrading, or manpower development.

PROFESSIONAL SKILLS

Test Administration	Data Analysis	Job and Interest Analysis
Public Speaking	Assessment of Needs	Vocational Counseling
Problem Solving	Career Counseling	Program Evaluation
Program Development	Group Facilitating	Grant Writing

PROFESSIONAL EXPERIENCES

* Designed, coordinated, and implemented career guidance programs for middle school youngsters, high school students, and adults.

* Authored career guidance materials that have received national distribution.

* Served as a career education consultant on local, county, and state levels.

* Taught career units which have experienced considerable popularity, evidenced by continually high enrollments.

* Presented seminars on local, state, and national levels on a variety of topics related to career development and personal growth.

* Experienced counselor with expertise in individual and group counseling and in personal and vocational areas.

* Recipient of outstanding educator award.

EDUCATION

MA   Wayne State University   1975
      Guidance and Counseling

BS   Wayne State University   1970
      Major: English

EMPLOYMENT

1976-1982   L'Anse Creuse Public Schools - Counselor
1971-1976   South Lake Public Schools - English teacher and part-time Career Counselor

RESUMES

(Example of a Functional Resume)

MYRNA L. SCHMUCKER

324 North Plain Avenue   Mount Hollins, MI 48043
Telephone (313) 000-0000

OBJECTIVE

I am seeking an administrative position in the general area of program development and implementation. I would like to be challenged in this position with variety and responsibility.

AREAS OF APPLICATION:
Human Resources Development	Personal Development Counselor
Market Support Representative	Multi-media Development
Program Training	Community Program Director

QUALIFICATIONS

AREAS OF EXPERIENCE:
Program Development	Personnel Evaluation	Personal Counseling
Word Processing	Public Speaking	Program Training

EDUCATION:

EdM	Colorado State University	1979
BS	Western Michigan University	1973
	Administrative Internship in a Media Center.	

ACHIEVEMENTS

- Designed and directed the first high school Word Processing course in the State of Michigan.
- Developed a multi-media program for a Word Processing course, resulting in a doubling of course enrollment.
- Developed and applied an individual learning program to assist individuals in decision-making and prioritizing tasks. Greater than 90 percent success following application of this program.
- Authored an article on Word Processing.
- Guest speaker at American Word Processing Association.
- Coordinated a personnel evaluation program for City of Saint Clair Shores, Michigan. Now in actual practice for second successful year.
- Counselor to handicapped individuals in training program, resulting in increased placements.
- General coordinator of nonprofit organization. Responsible for long-range program objectives, public relations, and executive decisions.

EMPLOYMENT

Business Education Instructor   Lakeview Public Schools   1974 to Present
     Business courses, program developer, curriculum committee member, supervisor of teacher aide, and sponsor of extra-curricular activities.

Adult Education Instructor   Imlay City Community Schools   1974
     Accounting I & II

Member: Michigan Society for Instructional Technology
          American Society for Training and Development

ALTERNATIVE CAREERS FOR TEACHERS

(Example of a Functional Resume)

LYNNE CUNNINGHAM
117 Beaconhill
Huntington, West Virginia 26003

Telephone (304) 000-0000

JOB OBJECTIVE: A public relations position involving program planning and coordination which requires an ability to work with diverse publics, develop publicity and promotional campaigns, and market services.

PROFESSIONAL SKILLS:

Writing	Program Development	Organizing
Public Speaking	Program Evaluation	Researching
Problem Solving	Group Facilitating	Typing
Consulting	Interviewing	Editing

PROFESSIONAL ACCOMPLISHMENTS:

* Organized a variety of successful community projects including fundraisers, community events, special projects, and award programs. The events have included media coverage, both newspapers and television.

* Experienced public speaker - presented programs on motivational techniques.

* Wrote instructional materials that have been distributed throughout the state.

* Edited for one year a monthly five page newsletter to foster improved community relations.

* Scriptwriter and director for video tape program to orient new patrons to services offered.

* Selected by peers to represent employees on Employer Council to improve the quality of work life. Efforts have resulted in improved communications and implementation of new ideas.

* Developed a publicity plan for a community group which increased membership 25% for two successive years.

* Designed and coordinated the public relations packets for two individuals in a contest. Entries were judged second in the nation and second in the state.

EDUCATION: MA University of West Virginia   1969
             BA University of Wisconsin   1965

EMPLOYMENT: Hale Public Schools, 6 years
             Pewa Public Schools, 5 years
             Hart Public Schools, 5 years

RESUMES

(Example of a Functional Resume)

MICHAEL MEREDITH
12 South Wilson
Tucson, Arizona 85712

Phone: (602) 000-0000

CAREER OBJECTIVE: I am seeking a position as a sales representative or manufacturer's representative. I desire a challenging position, one with variety and responsibility.

PROFESSIONAL EXPERIENCES:

- Sales Representative and consultant for Meissner, Inc. Duties are to supervise sales, make presentations, analyze and determine customer needs, recommend products, and further develop my territory.

- Created, developed, and marketed educational learning units.

- Independently worked in supervisory position for six years. Responsibilities included planning schedules and programs, motivating and evaluating participants.

- Experienced public speaker. Presentations made daily to groups of thirty.

- Organized, supervised, and motivated participants in several fund raising events. Profits increased by 30% each year.

- Served in liaison capacity between different groups and represented employer to community groups and individuals.

- Awarded outstanding service certificate by peers for contributions made both in the work environment and to fellow workers.

- Retail Sales — experienced in customer selection and sales, charges, cash transactions, and balancing daily totals.

EMPLOYMENT: Meissner, Inc. — Sales Representative — 1984 to present
Secondary Instructor — 6 years
National Sales — 2 years

EDUCATION: MA DEGREE — Indiana University

BA DEGREE — Ball State University

Major — Economics
Minor — Business Administration

165

ALTERNATIVE CAREERS FOR TEACHERS

(Example of a Functional Resume)

```
                        ALLISON ROBERTS
                     7302 E. Rocky Creek Place
                      Roselle, Illinois 60172

                      Phone:  (815) 000-0000
```

Objective: A position in sales with an established company where my strong skills in communication and interrelating with people will be of value.

Professional Skills

Public Speaking	Organizing	Program Planning
Negotiating	Motivating	Instructing
Problem Solving	Evaluating	Supervising

Professional Accomplishments

Planned, designed, and implemented a program in physical fitness for young adults which grew 600% in ten years. Personal skills contributing to this success were my motivational skills, problem-solving abilities, positive interpersonal relationships with participants, and my organizing and evaluating skills.

Selected by members to be honored as Jaycee of the Month for leadership efforts in organizing successful sales campaign.

Assisted in mediating and resolving grievances between employer and employee. Worked to establish improved relationships among employees, striving to bring a greater understanding and appreciation of the value and function of all.

Twice recipient of Outstanding Educator Award for contributions made to the profession, for fostering good community relations, and for cooperative work with colleagues.

Experienced public speaker. Presented workshops for adults and spoke as the keynote speaker at banquets.

Employment: Instructor and Coach, Stacy Public Schools, 10 years
             Instructor and Coach, Otsego Public Schools, 3 years
             Sales, part-time positions at different times in my
                  life in both retailing and insurance.

Education: MA   Loyola University, Illinois   1970
             BS   Illinois Central University   1963

References: Available upon request.

RESUMES

(Example of a Functional Resume)

JOHN HENRY
28882 Gill Drive
Lowell, Massachusetts 01851

Telephone: (413) 000-0000

OBJECTIVE: A director or management position in recreational leadership.

AREAS OF INTEREST:
- Hospital Recreation
- Camp Director
- Public Recreation
- Resort Recreation
- Employee Recreation Programs

EDUCATION: Lowell University, 10 hours in Recreational Leadership Boston College, BA degree in Physical Education 1974

EXPERIENCE:

- PLANNED, DESIGNED, and SUPERVISED a recreational program emphasizing life long sports for 720 young adults for ten years.

- COORDINATED recreational program to serve the community on Saturday mornings. Duties included ascertaining interests of participants, evaluating available facilities and equipment, scheduling participants, and creating an atmosphere to increase participation.

- RESEARCHED AND WROTE physical fitness programs for physically and mentally handicapped individuals.

- ARRANGED an INTERNSHIP for myself at Dells Resort, Maine assisting the director for four weeks.

- INSTRUCTED adults in aerobics and racquetball.

- CONSULTANT for the development of new programs in physical education and recreation.

- MANAGED recreational facilities for two summers at a summer camp which serviced vacationing families. Duties included ORDERING equipment, extensive RECORDKEEPING, ENCOURAGING participation, DEVELOPING programs, EVALUATING season's offerings, and DIRECTING the activities of the other recreational workers.

REFERENCES: Excellent references furnished upon request.

EMPLOYMENT: Ohio County Public Schools, Lowell, Massachusetts.

COVER LETTERS

Mailing a resume without a cover letter wastes postage, paper, and opportunity. A cover letter personalizes job seeking. Do not underestimate its importance. In three or four single-spaced paragraphs your cover letter should do three things:

(1) State your reason for sending the letter. "I am responding to the ad which appeared in the Sunday *Times* on April 22, 1985," or "Mary Smith, of your accounting department, suggested that I send you a resume," or "As per our conversation on Monday, May 8, I am forwarding a copy of my resume to you."
(2) Concisely state the position you are interested in and the expertise you offer. Be careful not to repeat everything you have already stated in the resume.
(3) End with a request for an interview.

When you are constructing the cover letter, make every effort to address it to a specific person, preferably to the person who will be doing the interviewing. A call to the company may provide you with the individual's name and title if you do not have this information. While phoning, verify the spelling of the name. Incorrect spelling of one's name is most offensive.

Tips for Writing Your Cover Letter

- Do not exceed one typed page.

- Avoid a form letter tone and appearance. Use the cover letter to express your personality.

RESUMES

- State that you would welcome the opportunity to interview, but do not press for a reply.

- Be concerned with the appearance of the letter. Do not undermine an outstanding letter with poor design and sloppy typing.

- Above all be positive. Avoid statements like "I have been teaching for twelve years and am now laid off," or "Having taught for twelve years, I wonder if my skills might be helpful to your company?"

When you finish your cover letter, assume the role of the employer and read it with a critical eye. What vibes do you get from the letter? Have you projected those aspects of yourself that you really want to project? Whether writing a cover letter, interviewing for information, or interviewing for a job, be positive. Convey enthusiasm for new challenges.

The effort you put into preparing your resume — your advertising package — will assist you in identifying transferable skills as you begin to market yourself. The research you do into career options influences which qualifications you highlight in your ad. All of this work is necessary. You need to express clearly where you're going and what you're taking along, if you intend to get there at all.

As you send out letters and resumes, develop a three-by-five-inch card file to keep track of them. You may wish to record the information in a way similar to this:

ALTERNATIVE CAREERS FOR TEACHERS

Date Sent: Person's Name:
                                             Title:
                                        Company:
                                          Address:

Job Sought:

Sent resume in response to:

Response to resume and follow-up:

8.

MARKETING STRATEGIES

Marketing, in this case, means procuring a job.

A noted marketing expert, Malcolm P. McNair, defines marketing as "the creation and delivery of a standard of living."[1] It is more than mere selling or advertising; his philosophy of marketing focuses on the economic welfare of a total society. Good marketing is good business; it's mutually beneficial. This broad definition can be applied to a career change. Your self-assessment endeavors and research into the world of work have clarified your skills and new career options. These efforts were essential to prepare you for the next step—target marketing your skills. You are now ready to deliver your skills to a new position.

To deliver implies considerably more action than to advertise. Your marketing strategies need to be active, to encompass more than just an advertising campaign. The real truth in McNair's definition is that you are not just going to create and deliver, or obtain, a new job for yourself. In fact, you will be delivering your skills to enhance your next employer's operation while enhancing your standard of living, too. Your standard of living includes not only income but also personal satisfaction, health, and professional and personal associates.

Delivering a standard of living, a new career, well deserves all the time and energy you can devote. Time spent in developing your total marketing program is a valuable investment in yourself.

---

[1] Malcolm P. McNair, "Marketing and the Social Challenge of Our Times," in Keith Cox and Ben M. Enis, eds., *A New Measure of Responsibility for Marketing* (Chicago: American Marketing Association, 1968).

ALTERNATIVE CAREERS FOR TEACHERS

What do you have to offer an employer? Your search should have provided you with the answers to this question as well as confidence in your marketability. This search was the first part of your marketing program. You now need to decide on target marketing strategies. This chapter will assist you in that task.

PREPARING FOR MARKETING

We are probably all in agreement that the cart does not work well if placed before the horse. Therefore, before you attempt to write the last part of your marketing program, evaluate how successfully you have composed the first part. If you can answer the following questions with some degree of confidence and certainty, begin developing a target marketing plan.

- Have you identified skills that you possess and desire to market?
  —Have you a broadened view of the skills you possess?
  —Are you convinced these skills are transferable?
  —Can you visualize yourself transferring your skills?

- Have you researched the world of work sufficiently to identify positions that require the skills you possess?
  —Have you broadened your view of where you can use your skills?
  —Do you have enthusiasm and confidence in your ability to perform work outside teaching?
  —Have you related options to yourself—to your interests, to the work environments you desire?

- Have you developed a networking system?
  —Have you told everyone you know, and then some, what new careers you are interested in?

MARKETING STRATEGIES

—Have you used your networking system to learn more about the jobs you have identified and to broaden further your insights and options?

- Have you composed, at least in rough form, an advertisement, your resume?
  —Have you practiced using action words when describing your accomplishments?
  —Can you write achievements or personal experiences so that they appear as dynamic as they are?
  —Have you shared your resume with others to obtain suggestions?

SOURCES OF JOB LEADS

Your goal now will be to identify the specific places that employ individuals in the job you desire and then to obtain interviews. The ultimate goal is, of course, delivery of a new position, one of your choosing.

While there are many avenues to that ultimate goal, some approaches have higher known success rates than others. You ought to be knowledgeable about all the approaches and then select a combination of those with which you feel most comfortable. Make sure your plan requires your active involvement—telephone calls, personal contacts—as opposed to sitting and waiting for things to happen. Work to open new doors; expect them to open and they will.

The following sources of job leads can be used both to identify specific places (companies, organizations, associations, businesses) and to obtain interviews:

Networking

The personal contacts that you have developed, your network, is the single best means of obtaining an interview and in many cases the actual position. It is your greatest resource. Use it! Don't be embarrassed. Employers will tell you they need good employees and, in fact, have trouble finding them. You have outstanding skills to sell and will be offering the employer a "fantastic find."

If you have developed a card file of your contacts and if you have used many of these people in interviewing for information, you already can identify those who will be most helpful in notifying you of openings and in helping you to obtain interviews. Keep in contact with them. Without making a nuisance of yourself, continue to apprise them of your interest.

Be sure to follow up every lead given to you. You never know which one of these will be the glass slipper. Often success begins as an unpromising lead.

Professional Associations and Publications

Most memberships in professional societies are open not only to practitioners but also to those with an interest in the area. Capitalize on this by joining the local association and attending their meetings. This is a golden opportunity to learn more about the field, to stay abreast of new developments, to meet and socialize with individuals employed in the field, and to expand your networking.

Local associations can be identified by writing to the national or parent organization. Many of the addresses are listed in Chapter 5 or can be obtained from your local reference librarian.

Membership in the national organization may also be advantageous. Many such associations publish journals which will increase your knowledge and aid you in learning the "buzz words," jargon, and acronyms of the profession. National associations frequently have available lists which can be used to identify employers. Some also operate placement services.

Identify all the professional publications that people read who hold the position you desire. Obtain copies to browse through; try your local library, college or university, or the reception area as you wait for an interview. Scan the journal to find possible employers and job listings.

Employment Agencies

Employment agencies are maintained by both private and public sectors of our society.

Public employment services are free and are maintained by state governments. The Federal Job Service Center is a good source of information on jobs with the United States Government. Local public employment centers frequently list nonprofessional, entry-level jobs or professional jobs with very small local companies.

Private employment agencies require a fee which is paid either by the employee, the employer, or both. Fees you pay may be deductible on your income tax. Many agencies specialize in a particular type of job; one may focus just on sales, another on management positions. Research and evaluate the agency before you enlist its help.

Private agencies can provide you with interviews leading to satisfying positions. They can also be very frustrating, time consuming, and ineffective. For a successful experience, you must have a clear idea of the type of position you desire and know that the agency has the ability to deliver interviews in that area. Be sure that you fully understand the method of payment and percent of commission.

Today's economy has affected the private agencies. Employers are receiving an enormous response for open positions. Some companies prefer reputable agencies to alleviate the workload of their personnel departments by prescreening applicants and arranging the interviews. Thus there are good jobs not available except through an agency.

If you choose to work through a private employment agency, you should:

(1) State clearly the position(s) you desire so that the agent will not waste your time with interviews for positions in which you have no interest.
(2) Make sure the agency has a market for the skills you desire to transfer.
(3) Develop a rapport with your agent.
(4) Feel free to work with more than one agency.
(5) Keep in touch with your agents at regular intervals.

College Placement Offices

Sources of professional jobs include college and university placement offices. Often you can pay a fee and receive their weekly or biweekly publication, even if not a graduate of that institution. This is most helpful if you live far away from the institution awarding your degree. If you are in an area where there are several colleges or universities, consider coordinating the subscriptions among interested colleagues and sharing the bulletins. There will likely be many applicants for the jobs listed in these bulletins. If the competition seems keen, remember that you have refined and developed the skills you wish to market. Do not underestimate your ability to compete.

The college or university placement office can also be an excellent source of additional information on specific companies. Prior to an interview you need to obtain an overall picture of the company, and the placement office is one source of this information.

MARKETING STRATEGIES

Newspaper Ads

Newspaper want ads list a very small percentage of the openings in any given city and an even smaller percentage of professional jobs. If you choose to use this source for leads, be sure to:

(1) Determine which is the "in" paper and which day is used by area business people to advertise openings.
(2) Read the ad carefully. Does your resume document stated requirements? If not, can you effectively treat them in the cover letter or will you need to rewrite the resume?

Mass Mailings

A very expensive and time-consuming approach is to mass-mail resumes and cover letters to numerous companies. This is done without contacts or networking and reaps few benefits and lots of anxiety as you await the mail carrier every day for the reply that seldom comes.

Creative Approach

Another means of obtaining a satisfying position is Bolles'[2] creative approach (see page 35). This approach involves extensive use of networking and interviewing for information to discover what problems an employer has that you can solve. Once you've gathered data and understood a problem, and analyzed how you can solve it, you then create a proposal defining what

---

[2] Richard Nelson Bolles, *What Color Is Your Parachute? A Practical Manual for Job Hunters and Career Changers* (Berkeley, CA: Ten Speed Press, 1984).

you can do for the employer. Thus you market your skills into a career that you desire, while serving the identified needs of an organization. All employers need problem solvers. An employer who has no openings may create one for you.

INTERVIEWING

Your marketing plan is proving successful. You find that personal initiative in pursuing leads has enabled you to schedule a job interview. An interview is not an offer of employment, so continue following and creating other job leads.

The Boy Scout motto, "Be Prepared," is an excellent one to adopt for your interview. Employers adept at interviewing will have done their homework and reviewed your resume prior to your arrival. They will also have identified traits and skills that they hope to secure in the new employee. You, too, need to prepare by doing research on the company that is interested in you.

Prior to the interview, find out as much as you can about the position and the company or organization. The source of the job lead may be helpful. The following resources may also be able to aid your investigation:

(1) A local stockbroker can provide you with reports on the company.
(2) Bankers can provide you with a Dun and Bradstreet report on the company.
(3) The local librarian can direct you to these references:
Standard and Poors' *Directory of Directors*
National Advertising Register
Dun and Bradstreet's *Million Dollar Directory* and *Middle Market Directory*
Thomas' *Register of American Manufacturing*
Directories listing companies by industry or geographical area

MARKETING STRATEGIES

Finding out as much as possible about the company and the position prior to the interview will increase your confidence, assist you in asking pertinent questions during the interview, and indicate your interest and initiative.

Tips for Interviewing

- Be yourself, confident in your abilities and enthusiastic for new challenges.

- Be positive. Don't express your pet peeves or discuss negative reactions to past employment.

- Get the name and title of those with whom you interview. The names of the secretaries can also be most helpful and aid your follow-up.

- Don't smoke unless invited to do so.

- Be on time.

- Dress neatly and appropriately.

- List ahead of time the five worst questions you could be asked in the interview and develop your responses.

- Feel free to ask questions but don't interrogate the interviewer.

- Don't call the interviewer by first name unless you are asked to do so.

- Be knowledgeable about the salary range appropriate for the job. Don't price yourself over or under market value.

- Be aware that the first few minutes of the interview are very important and set the tone for the rest of the interview. Be sure to make good eye contact.

Use your interviews as learning experiences. Evaluate and keep notes on them. If you are invited for a follow-up interview the notes may be very helpful. Compliment yourself for the areas you did well in and give thought to ways to improve the weaker ones. Permit yourself to grow and learn with each interview.

Expect some anxiety as you wait for the outcome of the interview. Stay positive and always continue investigating new job leads.

Follow up each interview with a concise thank-you letter to each individual who participated in the interview process. Two or three short paragraphs are ample. Express your appreciation for their time and interest and state your feelings regarding the possible position. A sample letter is included. It is only for illustration; you need to make every effort to personalize your letter to avoid a form letter appearance.

Be positive; believe in yourself and your ability to learn and to be trained. Imagine yourself being successful in the position you desire and soon it will not be make-believe. Commitment is the key. Devote your time, talents, and resources to making a successful career change. Develop a marketing plan and evaluate its effectiveness continually. You cannot accomplish the task in one quick leap; it's a little like climbing a mountain. It must be done step by step.

MARKETING STRATEGIES

Interview Follow-Up Letter

46201 Fairchild Road
Mt. Clemens, Michigan 48045
April 22, 1982

Mr. Jay Alexander
District Sales Manager
Books Unlimited
321 Riverfront Drive
Detroit, Michigan 48124

Dear Mr. Alexander:

Thank you for the courtesies and kindnesses extended to me during our interview on April 20.

The interview confirmed and heightened my enthusiasm for employment prospects with Books Unlimited. I see many challenging opportunities in the position and would welcome the chance to become a contributing member of your sales staff.

Again, my sincerest thanks for your interest in me. I look forward to hearing from you.

Sincerely,

Nancy Clark

Nancy Clark

9.

SETTING THE STAGE

FOR CHANGE

Change is a process, not an event. In this era of instantaneous everything — potatoes, pudding, advertised pain relief — we tend to want instant solutions to problems. Yet, for most of us, a career change is more than the event of landing a new job. It is a process that involves thoughtful analysis, time, evaluation, challenge, new experiences, and learning. There are no instant solutions or magic answers.

The career change process can be defined. By understanding the stages of career change, you better perceive your situation. You can determine where you are within the process, can see where you've been and the distance yet to go. This awareness enables you to identify some personal first steps in a program of action leading toward your goal of a new career.

A CAREER PLANNING MODEL

The career planning model illustrated here presents an overview of the career change process. Central to that process is the goal of establishing a new career. The stages before reaching that goal include:

A CAREER PLANNING MODEL FOR EDUCATORS SEEKING NEW ALTERNATIVES

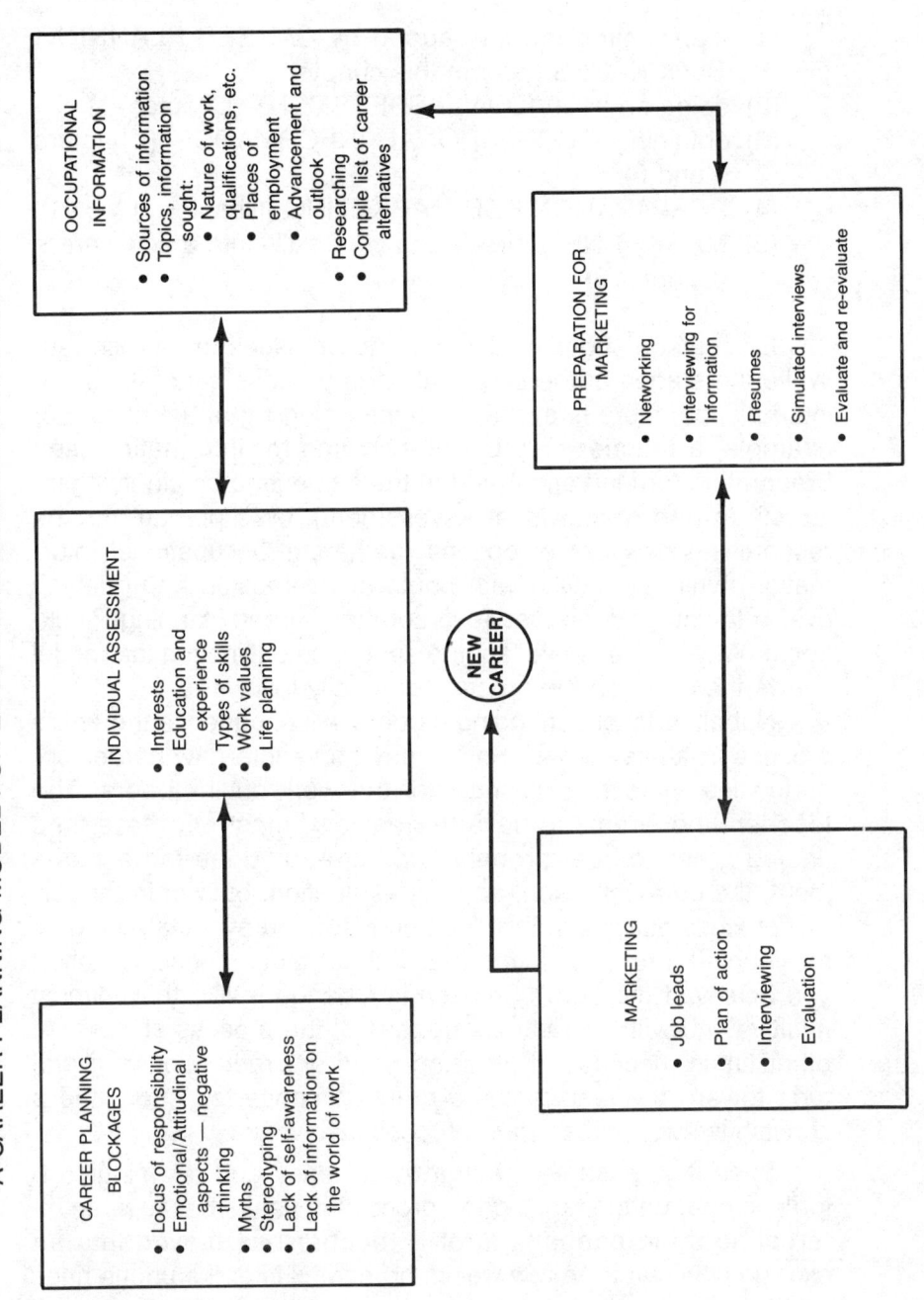

OCCUPATIONAL INFORMATION
- Sources of information
- Topics, information sought:
  - Nature of work, qualifications, etc.
  - Places of employment
  - Advancement and outlook
- Researching
- Compile list of career alternatives

INDIVIDUAL ASSESSMENT
- Interests
- Education and experience
- Types of skills
- Work values
- Life planning

CAREER PLANNING BLOCKAGES
- Locus of responsibility
- Emotional/Attitudinal aspects — negative thinking
- Myths
- Stereotyping
- Lack of self-awareness
- Lack of information on the world of work

PREPARATION FOR MARKETING
- Networking
- Interviewing for Information
- Resumes
- Simulated interviews
- Evaluate and re-evaluate

MARKETING
- Job leads
- Plan of action
- Interviewing
- Evaluation

NEW CAREER

(1) overcoming inertia caused by CAREER PLANNING BLOCKAGES (later in this chapter)
(2) doing an INDIVIDUAL ASSESSMENT (Chapter 4)
(3) obtaining OCCUPATIONAL INFORMATION (Chapters 5 and 6)
(4) PREPARATION FOR MARKETING (Chapter 7)
(5) MARKETING yourself and your skills into a new career (Chapter 8)

Each stage suggests things to do or issues to be resolved. While the stages of the career change process generally occur in sequence, there is overlap and intermingling of activities. For example, a teacher may be interviewing for information (see Preparation for Marketing) and at the same time be clarifying interests (a part of Individual Assessment). Or a person may be researching new career options (gathering Occupational Information) while struggling with bouts of depression and grieving over a lay-off and job loss (overcoming Career Planning Blockages). While there is overlap, the sequence outlined in the model shows the direction the process generally follows.

Not all teachers changing careers will experience the entire process in all its stages. Some may move into new career opportunities without doing much of the work outlined here. The teacher who seems to have the easiest, most effortless time finding a new career probably had already done the assessment, the data collection, and the evaluation, but not in the formal process outlined in this chapter. Have you ever stated a goal for yourself, and then found that without much conscious effort you achieved the goal? Sometimes change is like that, almost intuitive and without clear awareness of the process at work. At other times, because of pressing need or urgency or your attitude toward the task, change requires concerted effort and a conscious awareness of the process involved.

Even if your career change is an easy and seemingly effortless one, understanding the process is useful because an interesting thing happens after a teacher has moved into an exciting new career. A few weeks or months later the phone rings and a former teaching colleague, or a teacher friend of a friend, starts asking questions about making the change from educa-

SETTING THE STAGE FOR CHANGE

tion. Questions like, "How did you go about it? What opportunities did you find? How do personnel people really react to teachers? What tools or strategies helped? Any suggestions for me? I'm in a situation where . . . ." By understanding the career change process outlined in this chapter, you are better equipped to assist those teachers who follow you and who may call upon you for advice. And those calls will come!

CAREER PLANNING BLOCKAGES

Most of the obstacles barring the way of a teacher's successful career change are internal. They are barriers that are, for the most part, self-constructed and which keep one immobilized. Overcoming these barriers and the inertia they cause is the first step in making a career change. Norman Vincent Peale, renowned author of books on the power of positive thinking, wrote that the one person who had given Norman Vincent Peale the most trouble over the years had been Norman Vincent Peale!

CAREER PLANNING
BLOCKAGES

- Locus of responsibility
- Emotional/Attitudinal aspects — negative thinking
- Myths
- Stereotyping
- Lack of self-awareness
- Lack of information on the world of work

This is true, too, for most of us, perhaps all of us. We tend to be defeated, to have our progress obstructed, by ourselves. Not everyone will encounter career planning blockages. Information about them is presented so that the person who does encounter a blockage may be helped to recognize what is happening. By understanding a career planning blockage, its negative impact can be minimized.

Locus of Responsibility

One blockage involves the locus of responsibility. The responsibility for your career belongs with you. Sometimes when we dread facing a problem, we tend to connect it with something outside our control. We thus excuse ourselves from responsibility for the problem. Children in school do this when in trouble. They may blame a classmate for their own inattention or aggressiveness. They may blame their teacher or parents for their own underachieving and poor performance.

Blaming is a clear signal that ownership for a problem is being given up, that the individual is holding himself helpless and not responsible. A warning light should come on if you find yourself doing this with regard to your career change.

- "I'm too old. My age won't permit me to find a good job now."

- "The want ads don't have any jobs that appeal to me or for which I'd be qualified."

- "What can I do? I have too much education in the wrong field. My high school counselor gave me terrible advice."

Since you can't change your age, your history, or the workings of most institutions and organizations, giving them responsibility for your career situation keeps you stuck where you are. If you assign responsibility for your career change to something outside yourself, you lead yourself to feeling helpless, to inertia instead of action. You effectively give up control thus losing the power associated with being in control.

Accept your career planning as your own and actively search for a meaningful, rewarding position. Keep the locus of responsibility with you. Use the want ads and agencies, but do so as a part of your overall marketing plan. Stop yourself from assigning blame and analyze whether or not there really is an external obstacle in your path. Permit no molehill to become an insurmountable mountain. Use positive thinking; negative thinking will block your path.

SETTING THE STAGE FOR CHANGE

Emotional and Attitudinal Blockages

Change naturally brings some stress and anxiety. Career change can be an emotionally trying time depending somewhat on the reason for leaving the field of education. Our research found that teachers leaving education due to either layoff or burnout more frequently had emotional feelings that tended to create blockages. The teachers leaving education due to layoffs enjoyed teaching and their layoff, after a large personal investment in training and years of dedicated work proved to be a significant personal loss. These teachers experienced grieving, a process with stages of its own. They had to work through the various stages of denial, anger, bargaining, depression, to a final acceptance of their loss and recognition of hope for a good life after teaching.

If your career change results from layoff, recognize your experience of loss. Permit yourself to work through the grieving process, feel your loss, and then recognize that there is life beyond teaching. Denying your loss, or allowing a continuing depression, will block your progress toward a new career. Grieve, and then move on. Remember that while you have given much, you have also gained much. You have much to offer and there is a market for your many skills. Find that market, and you'll find another satisfying career.

For the teacher who leaves education because of stress and burnout, anger and resentment seem the strongest emotions. The helping professions, which include teaching, are considered high burnout occupations. These professions can take a severe toll on a dedicated individual. If you believe you are in serious need of a change, accept that need for a change and take steps to make one. It is OK to want to change occupations. Stay positive and do something positive for yourself. You can change careers and you will likely find, like others before you, a rewarding, more enjoyable lifestyle and healthier, happier career life outside of education.

The former teachers who experienced the easiest transition emotionally from education to other work were those who created their own career changes while simply in pursuit of new interests or rewards not available in teaching. Their career changes seemed more relaxed and gradual. Some occurred over a span of years through summer employment or volunteer work.

Regardless of the reason for your career change, by maintaining control of the career change process — by accepting yourself and acting responsibly in your own behalf — you choose self-enhancing behavior and act in an emotionally uplifting way. Strong emotional reactions or a negative attitude can create a blockage. Feelings can be either a blockage or they can be a signal that change needs to take place and a stimulus to positive action. Don't let emotions or attitude block your progress. It is more effective to maintain a positive attitude as much as possible and to provide yourself with emotional support (see Chapter 3). The transition to a new career will then be faster and easier.

Erroneous Beliefs, Impediments, Myths

Myths abound about teachers, teaching, and the world of work. Accepting some myths as truths can cause inertia. It is a myth that:

- Myth: Every job requires a particular set of talents.
  Truth: Most jobs can be done using a variety of talents. The higher the level of skill employed on a job, the more freedom an individual has to create his/her own style for doing the job.

- Myth: Business does not want or need the skills that teachers possess.
  Truth: Teachers possess some of the hottest, most transferable skills in demand in the business world today. (Public speaking, organizing, writing, and managing.)

- Myth: People who can, do! Others teach.

SETTING THE STAGE FOR CHANGE

Truth: Teaching requires the exercise of many sophisticated skills, particularly in the areas of working with people and data. Teaching and instructing mean *doing* a whole lot!

- Myth: A teacher needs new credentials, retraining, to get a start in a new career.
 Truth: Very few occupations require the specialized certificates of teaching. Teachers, through their education and experience, possess valuable skills and talents which ARE marketable into new careers. They don't need new credentials to move into most careers.

- Myth: It is vocationally immature to change jobs, let alone careers.
 Truth: Career development is often promoted by changing jobs, fields, or making lateral transfers in order to gain experience and access to paths of career advancement. It's often smart to make a job change.

- Myth: You can't get another good job directly from teaching.
 Truth: There are many alternative careers accessible directly from teaching.

If you believe that there are no jobs out there for which you qualify, you will act accordingly and will find no jobs out there. Guard that you do not accept a myth as a truth, thus creating a blockage which can keep you immobilized.

Stereotyping works much the same way to create a career development blockage. By seeing people or career fields in only a narrow, restricted view, one loses the clearer vision and understanding available through honest, open examination. Stereotypes which might impede a teacher's development of new career options include:

- Teachers can only teach.

- Women belong in maternal, nurturing types of occupations.

- Successful businesspeople are cold, ruthless, and greedy.

- Sales agents are manipulative, insincere, aggressive.

Stereotyping causes one to restrict investigation of opportunities within a new field because of narrow perceptions or preconceived notions.

Sound career planning requires an openness to looking at yourself and at new options. Myths and stereotypes, erroneous thinking about teachers, their abilities, and the world of work, can impede the process. Examine your beliefs about teachers and the world of work. Then don't let a myth or stereotype stand in your way or restrict your options.

Information Blockages

A teacher wanting to change careers needs information to see other alternatives. A lack of self-awareness or a lack of information on the world of work can be a blockage. Teachers confined to classrooms lack exposure to other occupations where their skills are in demand. Yet teachers also demonstrate continually the ability to gather information, to assess and evaluate, and to solve problems. As instructors, they are information experts. Overcoming an information blockage should be relatively easy; the skill is there. Recognize that if a lack of personal awareness or career information is preventing you from making your career change, then obtaining this information is the place to start.

SETTING THE STAGE FOR CHANGE

ACTION STAGES OF CAREER CHANGE

Individual Assessment

The action stages of the career planning model include the work explained in previous chapters. Individual assessment comes first because an individual needs some understanding of his interests, educational and experiential qualifications, marketable skills, and work values if he is to find a satisfying and fulfilling career. Any reader who is vague about his own interests, skills, values and significant experiences should return to Chapter 4 and do some work there to discover more about himself. Self-awareness generated by this self-assessment will enable the reader to focus his search for a new career and to more efficiently sift through and analyze the information about the more than 20,000 occupations in the United States. It helps to know what you want before you go searching for it.

INDIVIDUAL ASSESSMENT

- Interests
- Education and experience
- Types of skills
- Work values
- Life planning

Occupational Information

Obtaining occupational information is the next action stage in the career change process. The goals of this research are: (1) to expand your career options, (2) to gather data with which to analyze options in terms of your interests, skills, qualifications, needs and values, (3) to gain insights and background information useful in developing resumes and in marketing. To accomplish these goals you must: know where to find occupational information and gain access to these resources; know what information to look for; do the research; and then compile a list of career alternatives along with some data about each. Chapter 5 provides information on some career alternatives for teachers, organized by area of teacher certification, and offers sources of additional data. Chapter 6, "Occupational Research" provides directions to the most widely used and readily available sources of published occupational information. If you have some self-awareness and are ready to research career alternatives, start with the resources suggested in these two chapters. Your search for occupational information will lead from library to community as you seek more complete information on careers of interest. When you get to this point, you will be completing the occupational research stage and also beginning the next stage of the career change process.

OCCUPATIONAL INFORMATION

- Sources of information
- Topics, information sought:
  - Nature of work, qualifications, etc.
  - Places of employment
- Advancement and outlook
- Researching
- Compile list of career alternatives

Preparation for Marketing

Preparation for marketing is the stage where three important things happen. First, the awareness of self and occupational information are drawn together and focused on potential

SETTING THE STAGE FOR CHANGE

new careers. Secondly, reality testing takes place as the individual starts meeting and talking with people who work in the jobs being explored, thus testing the resume, interest level, and accuracy of research data. Thirdly, these discussions enable one to learn about current job market conditions, trends and developments locally which may suggest employment opportunities.

You accomplish this preparation for marketing by networking to conduct informational interviews (see Chapter 6) and by development of a resume which targets the career(s) you seek and highlights your demonstrated ability and the skill to perform the job. Your original research will provide contacts who can critique your resume, and prepare you — by providing insights, current knowledge, and practice in interviewing — for the actual marketing and job interviewing of the next stage. By way of illustration, an English teacher recently researching careers in advertising learned much from an informational interview. He learned that advertising copywriters maintain their own "books" (portfolios), with various samples of their writing (straight copy, radio scripts, TV scripts, dialogue) for presentation at job interviews. The teacher was given suggestions for creating a basic "book" and was offered the opportunity of a second interview and a critiquing of his samples. His experience reaffirmed that there are many gracious people willing to share valuable time and information with teachers.

PREPARATION FOR MARKETING

- Networking
- Interviewing for Information
- Resumes
- Simulated interviews
- Evaluate and re-evaluate

Throughout this preparation for the marketing stage the information about yourself and about occupations will be evaluated and re-evaluated. Avenues will become more apparent into a chosen field. When finished you will have some clearly defined and obtainable career goals and will have the draft of an appropriate resume relating yourself to each goal. You will also have had some practice at interviewing, made personal contacts and a few new friends, and possibly received some potential job leads to pursue.

Marketing

Considerable work has taken place before you get to the stage of actual job seeking or marketing. The goal of this stage is to receive an offer of employment in a new career. Marketing your skills involves demonstrating to those who need your skills that you have the ability to master the required tasks of a job. Your awareness of yourself and your skills, your knowledge of the world of work and its needs, and your understanding of the relationship between the two have prepared you to market your abilities into a new career. The action here involves developing and following up on job leads, letter writing and phone calling, tapping many sources of referral in your network of people and your community, applying and interviewing for jobs, and continually evaluating the process to strengthen job seeking skills. The leads will come. Rounds of interviews will follow and develop into offers of employment in a new career — goal accomplished.

```
        MARKETING

  • Job leads        • Interviewing

  • Plan of action   • Evaluation
```

SETTING THE STAGE FOR CHANGE

GETTING STARTED

At the end of the career change process there is a clear, measurable outcome, a new career. Getting from here to there requires a plan. Athletes prepare to win by following conditioning programs and game plans. Companies prepare to grow and flourish by developing plans and programs. People prepare for enjoyable vacations with plans. Teachers prepare good lessons with plans. Getting to a new career requires a plan.

Your own career change program will be designed to take you from your present stage in the career change process to a new career. Your program will include subgoals and steps to reach each subgoal. Think of it as climbing the stairs of a building. The building has many floors and some landings between the floors. You make the climb one step at a time. What happens, though, if a step is missing or you miss a step? What happens if you try to skip many steps altogether or jump a floor? If it is important to reach the top, it is important to build in all the floors and all the steps.

We suggest that you use the career planning model presented earlier to identify intermediate goals (the floors in your plan). Then, build steps to reach each of these goals. For example, if you are at the stage of needing self-assessment, your first staircase might focus on skills and look like the model on the following page:

My immediate goal: _To identify more clearly my skills_

1. Get paper and pencil and sit down at table
2. Do skills checklist in Chapter 4
3. Write three accomplishments and analyze for skills involved
4. List skills in order of importance and ability
5. Plan lunch with a friend to gain feedback and input
6.

SETTING THE STAGE FOR CHANGE

By breaking a project down into smaller stages and steps, it becomes more manageable. Sometimes a project can seem so enormous that the sheer magnitude of the endeavor stands in the way and stops a person. Painting a room can be like that. It's a project that you'd quickly like to have over and done with, yet it involves so many operations — selecting paint, spackling holes, sanding, collecting the dropcloths, ladders, stirrers, brushes, rollers and pans, disassembling the light fixtures, etc. Soon the whole project is too huge to do today. And so procrastination wins. Big projects need to be broken down into manageable steps.

The first step especially should be bite size to ensure success. Once movement is begun, momentum develops to help maintain that progress. If any one step along the way seems too large, it can be broken down into smaller, more manageable steps. The career planning model and the program outlines you develop can be helpful to analyze progress and problems encountered along the way. Is a step missing or should a different step be tried?

Planning for success also means planning to avoid obstacles. Build into your program consideration for caution signs, anything that might get in the way. The paper and pencil skills assessment may not go well if done at the kitchen table, before dinnertime, with the children arriving home from school or play. Anticipating obstacles enables prudent planning to avoid them.

If you have decided to change careers, look at the career planning model and determine where you are within the process. Using the form that follows, identify a first goal and map out the steps involved in reaching it. Consider what obstacles, if any, might interfere and plan for them. Then take the first step and you will continue the search and the exciting journey toward a new career.

Godspeed!

My immediate goal: _____
_____

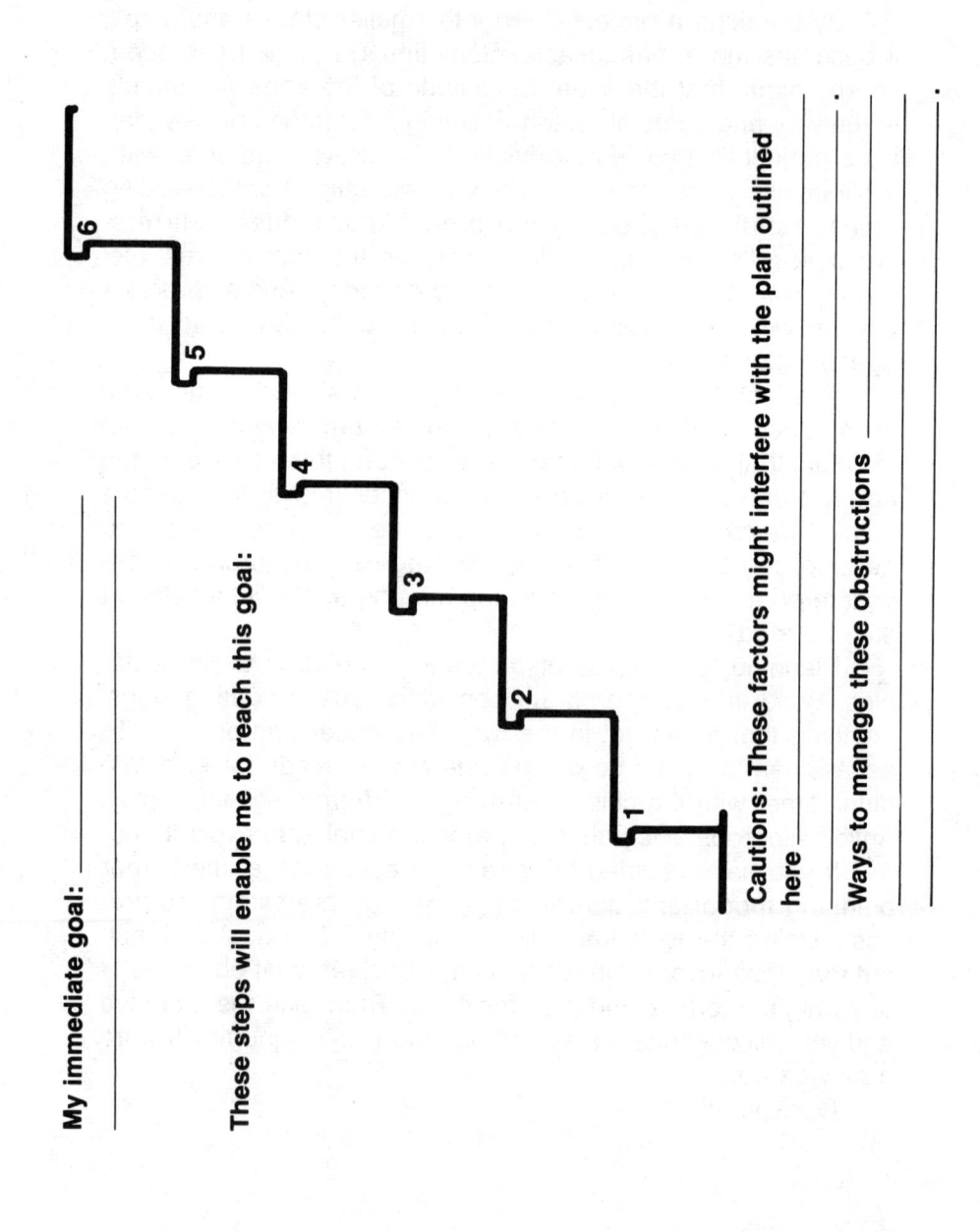

These steps will enable me to reach this goal:

1
2
3
4
5
6

Cautions: These factors might interfere with the plan outlined here _____
_____

Ways to manage these obstructions _____
_____

APPENDIX I.
JOBS IN THE FEDERAL GOVERNMENT BY COLLEGE MAJOR

This is a listing of the major fields of study which are considered valuable background for Government employment. Under each heading are a number of positions for which study in that field, or a pertinent specialization in that field, is particularly appropriate. This is just a representative sampling.

Any College Major

Administrative assistant
Alcohol and tobacco tax inspector
Alcohol, tobacco, and firearms special investigator
Budget officer
Budget analyst
Claims examiner
Computer specialist
Correctional officer
Criminal investigator
Customs inspector
Deputy U.S. marshal
Food program specialist
Immigration inspector
Import specialist
Industrial specialist
Intelligence research specialist

ALTERNATIVE CAREERS FOR TEACHERS

Internal security inspector
Investigator (General)
Management analyst
Museum curator
Narcotics agent
Personnel management specialist
Personnel staffing specialist
Public health program specialist
Public information specialist

Quality assurance specialist
Realty specialist
Revenue officer
Safety officer
Secret service agent
Supply management specialist
Tax law specialist
Veterans claims examiner
Writer and editor

Accounting

Accountant
Agricultural marketing specialist
Alcohol and tobacco tax inspector
Budget officer
Contract negotiator
Economist
Financial institution examiner
Industrial labor relations specialist

Internal revenue agent
Investigator (General)
Loan specialist
Special agent (IRS)
Supply management specialist
Tax law specialist
Traffic manager and traffic management specialist

Agriculture or Agricultural Services

Agricultural commodity grader
Agricultural management specialist
Agricultural marketing specialist
Agricultural market reporter

Animal husbandman
Entomologist
Hydrologist
Plant scientist (various branches)
Range conservationist
Realty specialist

APPENDIX I

Soil conservationist
Wildlife biologist

Anthropology (Social or Cultural)

Anthropologist
Sociologist

Archaeology

Anthropologist   Park ranger
Archaeologist

Architecture

Architect and marine   Realty specialist
  architect

Astronomy

Astronomer   Geodesist
Cartographer

Bacteriology

Microbiologist

ALTERNATIVE CAREERS FOR TEACHERS

Banking

Financial institution examiner
Investigator (General)

Loan specialist

Biology or Biological Sciences

Agricultural commodity grader
Agricultural management specialist
Animal husbandman
Biologist
Consumer safety inspector
Entomologist
Environmentalist
Fishery biologist
Geologist

Medical technologist
Microbiologist
Oceanographer
Park ranger
Pharmacologist
Physiologist
Plant scientist
Range conservationist
Statistician
Wildlife biologist
Zoologist

Botany

Entomologist
Forest products technologist
Hydrologist
Park ranger

Plant scientist
Range conservationist
Wildlife biologist

Business Administration

Administrative assistant
Agricultural commodity grader

Agricultural marketing specialist

APPENDIX I

Alcohol and tobacco tax inspector
Budget analyst
Contract negotiator
Financial institution examiner
Industrial relations specialist
Industrial specialist
Investigator (General)
Loan specialist
Park ranger
Personnel management specialist
Personnel staffing specialist
Printing and publications officer
Public health program specialist
Quality assurance specialist
Realty specialist
Revenue officer
Statistician
Supply management specialist
Tax law specialist
Traffic manager and traffic management specialist

Cartography

Cartographer

Chemistry

Agricultural commodity grader
Alcohol and tobacco tax inspector
Chemist
Compliance investigator
Consumer safety inspector
Fishery biologist
Forest products technologist
Geologist
Hydrologist
Medical technologist
Microbiologist
Oceanographer
Patent examiner
Pharmacologist
Quality assurance specialist

Commercial Art

Illustrator
Printing and publications officer

Visual information specialist

Dentistry

Dentist

Dietetics

Dietitian

Dramatic Arts

Recreation specialist

Economics

Agricultural commodity grader
Agricultural marketing specialist
Agricultural market reporter
Alcohol and tobacco tax inspector
Archivist
Budget officer

Economist
Financial institution examiner
Historian
Industrial relations specialist
Investigator (General)
Loan specialist
Operations research analyst
Printing and publications officer

APPENDIX I

Revenue officer
Sociologist
Statistician
Supply management
  specialist

Tax law specialist
Traffic manager and traffic
  management specialist

Education

Educator
Recreation specialist

Sociologist
Statistician

Engineering

Alcohol and tobacco tax
  inspector
Cartographer
Engineer (various branches)
Environmentalist
Forest products technologist
Geodesist
Geologist

Hydrologist
Industrial specialist
Meteorologist
Oceanographer
Patent examiner
Quality assurance specialist
Realty specialist
Statistician

English

Printing and publications
  officer

Public information specialist
Writer-Editor

ALTERNATIVE CAREERS FOR TEACHERS

Entomology

Entomologist

Finance

Alcohol and tobacco tax inspector
Financial institution examiner
Industrial relations specialist
Investigator (General)
Loan specialist
Realty specialist
Revenue officer
Tax law specialist
Traffic manager and traffic management specialist

Fine Arts

Illustrator
Recreation specialist
Visual information specialist

Fish and Game Management

Fishery biologist
Park ranger
Range conservationist
Wildlife biologist

Food Technology

Agricultural commodity grader
Consumer safety inspector

APPENDIX I

Forestry

Cartographer
Forester
Forest products technologist

Park ranger
Realty specialist

Geodesy

Cartographer
Geodesist

Meteorologist

Geography

Cartographer
Meteorologist

Oceanographer
Sociologist

Geology

Cartographer
Geologist
Geophysicist
Hydrologist
Meteorologist

Oceanographer
Park ranger
Range conservationist
Realty specialist

Geophysics

Cartographer
Geodesist
Geophysicist

Meteorologist
Oceanographer
Physicist

ALTERNATIVE CAREERS FOR TEACHERS

History

Archivist
Historian
Park ranger
Sociologist

Home Economics

Agricultural commodity grader
Home economist

Hospital Administration

Hospital administrative assistant
Public health program specialist

Hydrology

Hydrologist

Industrial Arts

Recreation specialist

Industrial Management

Administrative assistant
Budget analyst
Industrial relations specialist
Industrial specialist

APPENDIX I

Investigator (General)
Printing and publications officer
Quality assurance specialist
Supply management specialist

International Law or International Relations

Historian
Sociologist

Landscape Architecture or Design

Landscape architect

Languages (Modern)

Translator analyst

Law

Agricultural marketing specialist
Alcohol and tobacco tax inspector
Attorney
Contract negotiator
Criminal investigator
Investigator (General)
Loan specialist
Realty specialist
Revenue officer
Special agent (IRS)
Supply management specialist
Tax law specialist

Library Science

Librarian

Marketing

Agricultural commodity grader
Agricultural marketing specialist
Agricultural market reporter
Contract negotiator
Statistician
Supply management specialist

Mathematics

Agricultural marketing specialist
Astronomer
Cartographer
Chemist
Economist
Geodesist
Geologist
Geophysicist
Hydrologist
Mathematician
Meteorologist
Oceanographer
Operations research analyst
Statistician

Medical Illustration

Illustrator

APPENDIX I

Medical Record Library Science

Medical record librarian

Medical Technology

Medical technologist

Medicine

Medical officer (physician)
Pharmacologist

Metallurgy

Metallurgist
Quality assurance specialist

Meteorology

Cartographer	Meteorologist
Hydrologist	Oceanographer

Microbiology

Microbiologist

Music

Recreation specialist

Natural Sciences

Meteorologist
Oceanographer

Park ranger
Range conservationist

Nursing

Nurse

Occupational Therapy

Occupational therapist

Oceanography

Cartographer
Fishery biologist

Meteorologist
Oceanographer

Operations Research

Operations research analyst

APPENDIX I

Pharmacology

Pharmacologist

Pharmacy

Food and drug assistant   Pharmacologist
Pharmacist

Physical Education

Recreation specialist

Physical Sciences

Aerospace technologist   Meteorologist
Biomedical engineer   Oceanographer
Cartographer   Patent examiner
Chemist   Pharmacologist
Environmentalist   Physicist
Geophysicist   Statistician
Hydrologist

Physical Therapy

Physical therapist

Physics

Alcohol and tobacco tax inspector
Cartographer
Consumer safety inspector
Engineer
Forest products technologist
Geodesist
Geologist
Geophysicist
Hydrologist
Meteorologist
Oceanographer
Patent examiner
Physicist
Quality assurance specialist

Physiology

Pharmacologist
Physiologist

Police Administration or Law Enforcement

Border patrol agent
Criminal investigator
Customs inspector
Park ranger
Special agent

Political Science

Administrative assistant
Archivist
Budget officer
Historian
Industrial relations specialist
Personnel management specialist
Personnel staffing specialist
Sociologist

APPENDIX I

Psychology

Personnel management specialist
Personnel staffing specialist
Psychologist
Public health program specialist
Sociologist
Statistician

Public Administration

Archivist
Administrative assistant
Budget officer
Industrial relations specialist
Investigator (General)
Personnel management specialist
Personnel staffing specialist
Public health program specialist
Management analyst
Community planner
Hospital management specialist

Radio and Television Management

Recreation specialist

Range Management

Range conservationist

Recreation

Recreation specialist

Social Sciences

Investigator (General)
Park ranger
Personnel management
  specialist
Personnel staffing specialist
Realty specialist
Sociologist
Statistician

Social Welfare

Social work associate
Social worker
Sociologist

Sociology

Archivist
Personnel management
  specialist
Public health program
  specialist
Recreation specialist
Sociologist
Statistician

Speech

Speech pathologist and
  audiologist

Statistics

Argricultural marketing
  specialist
Economist
Loan specialist

APPENDIX I

Operations research analyst
Sociologist
Statistician

Supply management specialist
Traffic manager and traffic management specialist

Technology or Technical Curricula

Forest products technologist
Patent examiner

Quality assurance specialist

Transportation

Traffic manager and traffic management specialist

Veterinary Medicine

Pharmacologist
Veterinary medical officer

Visual Communications

Public information specialist
Visual information specialist

ALTERNATIVE CAREERS FOR TEACHERS

Zoology

Entomologist
Fishery biologist
Physiologist

Range conservationist
Wildlife biologist
Zoologist

APPENDIX II.

MATCHING PERSONAL AND JOB CHARACTERISTICS[1]

The following chart offers an overview of the entire world of work. It lists 281 occupations from the *Occupational Outlook Handbook* and matches them against twenty-three characteristics. The occupations are arranged in clusters; some groups are more related to a teacher's skills and interests than others.

If you recall that teachers have college degrees and are in the top 15 percent educationally, that they deal with data at a problem-solving level and with people at an instructional level, that they are skillful at persuading or motivating, and characteristically take much initiative in their work, the usefulness of this chart becomes clear. It identifies career alternatives and clusters of jobs where a teacher's skills can have application.

Our research has indicated that the former teachers least satisfied in new careers are those who have accepted underemployment. This chart can also help by defining the job realities of the options you may be considering. While there are many jobs in the working world that you may be qualified to do, not all of them draw on the high level of people and data skills you have developed.

Some explanatory notes appear at the end of the tables. A T under the Technical School/Apprenticeship training column

---

[1]This chart is reprinted from the *Occupational Outlook Quarterly*, the U.S. Department of Labor's Career Guidance Magazine, Fall 1978, Vol. 22, 2–13.

refers to technical or vocational school and an A denotes the availability of apprenticeship programs. Under the column headed college, a ± indicates that education beyond a bachelor's degree is required for entry-level positions.

APPENDIX II

	High school	Tech. schl/Apprenticeship trng.	Junior college	College	Problem-solving ability	Uses tools, machinery	Instructs others	Repetitious work	Hazardous	Outdoors	Physical stamina	Generally confined	Precision	Works with detail	Frequent public contact	Part-time	Able to see results	Creativity	Influences others	Competition on the job	Works as part of a team	Jobs widely scattered	Initiative
	1	2	3	4	5	6	7	8	9	10	11	12	13	14	15	16	17	18	19	20	21	22	23
INDUSTRIAL PRODUCTION AND RELATED OCCUPATIONS																							
Foundry occupations																							
Patternmakers	•	A			•						•	•	•				•				•		•
Molders		A			•			•	•		•	•					•				•		•
Coremakers		A			•			•			•	•					•				•		•
Machining occupations																							
All-round machinists	•	A			•	•			•			•	•	•			•				•		•
Instrument makers (mechanical)	•	A			•	•						•	•	•			•	•			•		•
Machine tool operators					•	•		•	•			•	•				•				•		•
Setup workers (machine tools)	•	A			•	•			•			•	•	•			•				•		•
Tool-and-die makers	•	A			•	•						•	•	•			•				•		•
Printing occupations																							
Compositors	•	A			•							•	•	•			•				•		•
Lithographers	•	A			•							•	•	•			•	•	•		•		•
Photoengravers	•	A			•							•	•	•			•				•		•
Electrotypers and stereotypers	•	A			•	•		•				•	•	•			•				•		•
Printing press operators and assistants	•	A			•	•		•	•			•	•				•				•		•
Bookbinders and bindery workers	•	A			•	•		•	•			•	•				•						•
Other industrial production and related occupations																							
Assemblers					•	•		•				•	•								•		•
Automobile painters		A			•	•			•		•	•					•				•		•
Blacksmiths		A			•	•	•		•		•						•	•			•		•
Blue-collar worker supervisors	•	(¹)	(¹)	(¹)	•		•						•						•		•	•	•
Boilermaking occupations		A			•	•			•	•	•		•				•				•		•
Boiler tenders						•		•		•	•												•
Electroplaters	•	A			•	•		•				•	•				•				•		•
Forge shop occupations	(²)	(²)			•	•	•		•		•						•				•		•
Furniture upholsterers					•	•			•		•						•	•					•
Inspectors (manufacturing)					•	•	•						•	•	•								•
Millwrights		A			•	•	•		•		•		•	•			•				•		•
Motion picture projectionists					•	•	•					•			•								•
Ophthalmic laboratory technicians	•				•	•						•	•								•		•
Photographic laboratory occupations					•	•						•	•								•		•
Power truck operators					•	•	•	•	•	•							•				•		•
Production painters					•	•		•	•	•							•				•		•
Stationary engineers		A			•	•			•		•		•				•				•		•
Waste water treatment plant operators	•	(²)	(²)	(²)	•	•			•	•		•	•				•				•	•	•
Welders	•	T			•	•		•	•	•	•						•				•		•

Notes appear at the end of the table

ALTERNATIVE CAREERS FOR TEACHERS

OFFICE OCCUPATIONS	1 High school	2 Tech. sch/Apprenticeship trng.	3 Junior college	4 College	5 Problem-solving ability	6 Uses tools, machinery	7 Instructs others	8 Repetitious work	9 Hazardous	10 Outdoors	11 Physical stamina	12 Generally confined	13 Precision	14 Works with detail	15 Frequent public contact	16 Part-time	17 Able to see results	18 Creativity	19 Influences others	20 Competition on the job	21 Works as part of a team	22 Jobs widely scattered	23 Initiative
Clerical occupations																							
Bookkeeping workers	•					•						•	•	•		•	•					•	•
Cashiers						•						•	•	•	•							•	•
Collection workers	•					•							•	•	•				•			•	•
File clerks						•								•			•					•	•
Hotel front office clerks	•				•	•						•	•	•	•							•	•
Office machine operators	•					•	•	•				•	•	•								•	•
Postal clerks	•					•		•				•		•								•	
Receptionists	•					•	•					•		•	•	•						•	
Secretaries and stenographers	•					•						•		•	•	•						•	
Shipping and receiving clerks				•		•	•							•								•	•
Statistical clerks	•					•						•	•	•								•	
Stock clerks				•		•								•								•	
Typists	•					•						•	•	•	•	•						•	
Computer and related occupations																							
Computer operating personnel	•	T		•	•	•						•	•	•								•	•
Programmers		(¹)	(¹) (¹)	•									•	•								•	•
Systems analysts			•	•	•								•	•									•
Banking occupations																							
Bank clerks	•					•						•	•	•								•	•
Bank officers and managers			•	•	•								•	•	•					•		•	•
Bank tellers						•						•	•	•	•							•	
Insurance occupations																							
Actuaries			•	•									•	•	•							•	
Claim representatives		(¹)	(¹)	•	•							•		•	•	•						•	•
Underwriters			•	•									•	•	•							•	•
Administrative and related occupations																							
Accountants			•	•									•	•	•							•	•
Advertising workers			•	•										•	•		•	•	•	•		•	•
Buyers			•	•										•					•	•	•	•	•
City managers			+	•	•									•	•		•		•		•	•	•
College student personnel workers			•	•	•									•	•				•			•	•
Credit managers			•	•	•									•	•				•			•	•
Hotel managers and assistants			•	•										•	•				•			•	•
Industrial traffic managers	(¹)	(¹)	(¹)	•										•					•			•	•
Lawyers			+	•		•								•	•		•	•	•			•	•
Marketing research workers			•	•									•	•				•				•	•
Personnel and labor relations workers			•	•	•									•	•		•		•			•	•

222

APPENDIX II

	High school	Tech. schl/Apprenticeship trng.	Junior college	College	Problem-solving ability	Uses tools, machinery	Instructs others	Repetitious work	Hazardous	Outdoors	Physical stamina	Generally confined	Precision	Works with detail	Frequent public contact	Part-time	Able to see results	Creativity	Influences others	Competition on the job	Works as part of a team	Jobs widely scattered	Initiative
	1	2	3	4	5	6	7	8	9	10	11	12	13	14	15	16	17	18	19	20	21	22	23
Public relations workers				•	•									•	•			•	•	•	•	•	•
Purchasing agents				•	•									•	•						•		•
Urban planners				+	•									•	•		•	•	•		•		•
SERVICE OCCUPATIONS																							
Cleaning and related occupations																							
Building custodians					•	•		•			•				•						•		
Hotel housekeepers and assistants					•	•		•			•			•	+						•		
Pest controllers					•	•	•		•		•			•							•		
Food service occupations																							
Bartenders								•	•		•			•	•						•	•	
Cooks and chefs		(²)	(²)		•			•	•		•	•		•		•	•				•	•	
Dining room attendants and dishwashers								•			•			•	•						•	•	
Food counter workers						•		•			•	•		•	•						•	•	
Meatcutters		A			•	•		•	•		•	•		•			•		•		•	•	
Waiters and waitresses						•		•			•			•	•						•	•	
Personal service occupations																							
Barbers		T			•	•		•			•	•		•	•	•	•				•		
Bellhops and bell captains						•		•			•			•	•						•		
Cosmetologists		T			•	•			•		•	•		•	•	•	•	•			•		
Funeral directors and embalmers	•	T		•	•				•		•			•	•		•				•		
Private household service occupations																							
Private household workers					•	•		•			•				•							•		
Protective and related service occupations																							
Correction officers	•				•		•	•	•		•	•	•							•	•	•	
FBI special agents			•	•	•		•		•	•	•		•	•	•					•	•	•	•
Firefighters	•			•	•	•			•	•	•		•		•						•	•	
Guards								•	•	•	•	•			•						•	•	
Police officers	•			•	•				•	•	•		•	•					•	•	•	•	
State police officers	•			•	•		•		•	•	•		•	•					•	•	•	•	
Construction inspectors (Government)	•	T			•	•			•	•	•			•	•						•	•	
Health and regulatory inspectors (Government)		(¹)	(¹)	(¹)	•		•		•				•	•	•						•	•	•
Occupational safety and health workers		(¹)	(¹)	•	•		•							•	•						•	•	•
Other service occupations																							
Mail carriers						•		•		•	•			•							•	•	

ALTERNATIVE CAREERS FOR TEACHERS

	High school	Tech. schl/Apprenticeship trng.	Junior college	College	Problem-solving ability	Uses tools, machinery	Instructs others	Repetitious work	Hazardous	Outdoors	Physical stamina	Generally confined	Precision	Works with detail	Frequent public contact	Part-time	Able to see results	Creativity	Influences others	Competition on the job	Works as part of a team	Jobs widely scattered	Initiative
	1	2	3	4	5	6	7	8	9	10	11	12	13	14	15	16	17	18	19	20	21	22	23
Telephone operators	•						•	•	•			•		•			•					•	
EDUCATION AND RELATED OCCUPATIONS																							
Teaching occupations																							
Kindergarten and elementary school teachers				•	•		•							•	•			•	•		•	•	•
Secondary school teachers				•	•		•							•	•			•	•	•	•	•	•
College and university teachers			+	•	•		•							•	•			•	•	•	•	•	•
Teacher aides	•						•							•	•	•					•	•	
Library occupations																							
Librarians			+	•	•		•							•	•			•	•		•	•	•
Library technicians and assistants	•	T					•							•	•	•						•	•
SALES OCCUPATIONS																							
Automobile parts counter workers	•					•	•				•				•							•	
Automobile sales workers	•														•	•			•	•		•	•
Automobile service advisors	•				•	•	•								•							•	•
Gasoline service station attendants						•	•	•	•	•	•				•	•						•	
Insurance agents and brokers	(¹)		(¹)	(¹)	•		•							•	•	•			•	•		•	•
Manufacturers' sales workers			•	•											•				•	•		•	•
Models							•				•				•					•	•		
Real estate agents and brokers	•	T		•	•		•							•	•	•			•	•		•	•
Retail trade sales workers	•						•	•			•			•	•	•			•	•	•		
Route drivers							•	•			•				•					•		•	•
Securities sales workers			•	•	•						•	•	•	•	•				•	•		•	•
Travel agents	•			•	•									•	•				•	•		•	•
Wholesale trade sales workers	•														•	•			•	•		•	•
CONSTRUCTION OCCUPATIONS																							
Bricklayers, stonemasons, and marble setters		A			•	•			•	•	•						•	•					•
Carpenters					•	•			•	•	•						•	•					•
Cement masons and terrazzo workers					•				•	•	•						•					•	•
Construction laborers					•				•	•	•											•	•
Drywall installers and finishers					•	•	•	•			•						•						•
Electricians (construction)	•	A			•	•			•	•	•	•					•						•
Elevator constructors	•				•	•			•		•						•						•
Floor covering installers					•	•	•				•						•						•
Glaziers	•	A			•	•			•	•	•	•					•					•	•
Insulation workers					•			•	•		•						•						•

224

APPENDIX II

	High school	Tech. sch/Apprenticeship trng.	Junior college	College	Problem-solving ability	Uses tools, machinery	Instructs others	Repetitious work	Hazardous	Outdoors	Physical stamina	Generally confined	Precision	Works with detail	Frequent public contact	Part-time	Able to see results	Creativity	Influences others	Competition on the job	Works as part of a team	Jobs widely scattered	Initiative
	1	2	3	4	5	6	7	8	9	10	11	12	13	14	15	16	17	18	19	20	21	22	23
Ironworkers						•			•	•	•						•					•	•
Lathers						•			•								•						•
Operating engineers (construction machinery operators)		T			•	•			•	•	•	•					•						•
Painters and paperhangers						•		•	•	•	•					•	•						•
Plasterers						•						•					•						•
Plumbers and pipefitters	•	A			•	•			•	•	•		•		•		•						•
Roofers						•			•	•	•	•					•						•
Sheet-metal workers	•	A			•	•				•		•	•				•						•
Tilesetters		A				•						•					•						•

OCCUPATIONS IN TRANSPORTATION ACTIVITIES

Air transportation occupations

Air traffic controllers	•	T			•		•					•	•	•							•	•	•
Airplane mechanics	•	T			•	•			•	•	•		•				•				•	•	
Airplane pilots	•	T			•	•						•	•								•	•	•
Flight attendants	•						•	•							•		•					•	
Reservation, ticket, and passenger agents	•				•		•	•					•		•	•						•	•

Merchant marine occupations

Merchant marine officers	•	T	•		•	•	•		•	•	•		•	•								•	•
Merchant marine sailors						•		•	•	•	•	•									•		

Railroad occupations

Brake operators	•					•		•	•	•	•										•	•	
Conductors	•				•		•	•	•												•	•	•
Locomotive engineers	•				•	•		•			•										•	•	
Shop trades		A			•	•			•	•	•										•	•	
Signal department workers					•	•			•			•			•						•	•	
Station agents					•		•	•				•		•	•						•	•	
Telegraphers, telephoners, and tower operators								•			•										•	•	
Track workers						•			•	•	•									•		•	

Driving occupations

Intercity busdrivers						•		•			•			•									•
Local transit busdrivers						•		•			•			•									•
Local truckdrivers						•		•			•												•
Long distance truckdrivers						•		•			•												•
Parking attendants						•		•	•	•	•					•	•						•
Taxicab driver						•		•		•						•	•						•

ALTERNATIVE CAREERS FOR TEACHERS

SCIENTIFIC AND TECHNICAL OCCUPATIONS	High school	Tech. sch/Apprenticeship trng.	Junior college	College	Problem-solving ability	Uses tools, machinery	Instructs others	Repetitious work	Hazardous	Outdoors	Physical stamina	Generally confined	Precision	Works with detail	Frequent public contact	Part-time	Able to see results	Creativity	Influences others	Competition on the job	Works as part of a team	Jobs widely scattered	Initiative
	1	2	3	4	5	6	7	8	9	10	11	12	13	14	15	16	17	18	19	20	21	22	23
Conservation occupations																							
Foresters				•	•					•	•	•										•	•	•
Forestry technicians		•				•				•	•	•										•	•	
Range managers				•	•					•	•	•										•	•	•
Soil conservationists				•	•		•			•												•	•
Engineers																							
Aerospace				•	•								•	•			•	•			•		•
Agricultural				•	•								•	•			•	•			•	•	•
Biomedical				•	•								•	•			•	•			•	•	•
Ceramic				•	•								•	•			•	•			•	•	•
Chemical				•	•	•							•	•			•	•			•	•	•
Civil				•	•								•	•			•	•			•	•	•
Electrical				•	•								•	•			•	•			•	•	•
Industrial				•	•								•	•			•	•			•	•	•
Mechanical				•	•								•	•			•	•			•	•	•
Metallurgical				•	•								•	•			•	•			•	•	•
Mining				•	•								•	•			•	•			•	•	•
Petroleum				•	•								•	•			•	•			•	•	•
Environmental scientists																							
Geologists				•	•	•				•	•			•	•			•			•		•	•
Geophysicists				•	•	•				•				•	•			•			•		•	•
Meteorologists				•	•	•								•	•			•			•		•	•
Oceanographers				+	•	•				•				•	•			•					•	•
Life science occupations																							
Biochemists				+	•	•								•	•			•					•	•
Life scientists				+	•	•								•	•			•			•		•	•
Soil scientists				•	•	•								•	•								•	•
Mathematics occupations																							
Mathematicians				•	•									•	•			•					•	•
Statisticians				•	•									•	•			•					•	•
Physical scientists																							
Astronomers				+	•	•								•	•			•					•	•
Chemists				•	•	•								•	•			•					•	•
Food scientists				•	•	•								•	•			•					•	•
Physicists				+	•	•								•	•			•					•	•
Other scientific and technical occupations																							
Broadcast technicians	•	T			•	•					•	•									•		
Drafters	•	T				•	•				•	•			•				•			•	•
Engineering and science technicians	•	T			•	•							•	•								•	•
Surveyors	•	T				•				•	•		•	•								•	•

226

APPENDIX II

	High school	Tech. sch/Apprenticeship trng.	Junior college	College	Problem-solving ability	Uses tools, machinery	Instructs others	Repetitious work	Hazardous	Outdoors	Physical stamina	Generally confined	Precision	Works with detail	Frequent public contact	Part-time	Able to see results	Creativity	Influences others	Competition on the job	Works as part of a team	Jobs widely scattered	Initiative
	1	2	3	4	5	6	7	8	9	10	11	12	13	14	15	16	17	18	19	20	21	22	23
MECHANICS AND REPAIRERS																							
Telephone craft occupations																							
Central office craft occupations					•	•		•				•		•			•					•	
Central office equipment installers					•	•		•			•	•		•			•					•	
Line installers and cable splicers					•	•		•	•	•		•										•	
Telephone and PBX installers and repairers					•	•		•			•				•							•	
Other mechanics and repairers																							
Air-conditioning, refrigeration, and heating mechanics	•				•	•		•									•					•	
Appliance repairers	•				•	•		•									•					•	
Automobile body repairers		A			•	•		•			•	•					•					•	
Automobile mechanics		A			•	•		•			•	•	•				•					•	
Boat-engine mechanics					•	•		•			•	•					•					•	
Bowling-pin-machine mechanics					•	•	•	•			•	•					•					•	
Business machine repairers	•	T			•	•		•					•				•					•	•
Computer service technicians	•	T			•	•		•					•	•			•					•	•
Diesel mechanics		A			•	•		•			•	•	•				•					•	
Electric sign repairers	•				•	•			•	•	•						•					•	
Farm equipment mechanics		A			•	•		•		•	•						•					•	
Industrial machinery repairers		A			•	•		•			•	•					•					•	
Instrument repairers	•	A			•	•						•					•					•	
Jewelers	•	A			•	•							•	•			•		•			•	•
Locksmiths					•	•							•	•			•					•	
Maintenance electricians	•	A			•	•		•			•						•					•	
Motorcycle mechanics					•	•		•				•					•					•	
Piano and organ tuners and repairers	•	T			•	•							•		•	•	•					•	
Shoe repairers						•		•	•			•					•					•	•
Television and radio service technicians		T			•	•		•					•	•			•					•	•
Truck mechanics and bus mechanics		A			•	•		•			•	•	•				•					•	
Vending machine mechanics					•	•		•	•								•					•	•
Watch repairers		T			•	•							•	•			•					•	•
HEALTH OCCUPATIONS																							
Dental occupations																							
Dentists				+	•	•	•					•			•		•		•			•	•
Dental assistants	•	T			•	•	•						•	•	•		•					•	•
Dental hygienists			•		•	•	•								•		•	•				•	•
Dental laboratory technicians	(³)	(²)			•	•		•					•				•					•	•
Medical practitioners																							
Chiropractors				+	•	•	•					•	•	•	•	•		•	•			•	•

227

ALTERNATIVE CAREERS FOR TEACHERS

	High school	Tech. sch/Apprenticeship trng.	Junior college	College	Problem-solving ability	Uses tools, machinery	Instructs others	Repetitious work	Hazardous	Outdoors	Physical stamina	Generally confined	Precision	Works with detail	Frequent public contact	Part-time	Able to see results	Creativity	Influences others	Competition on the job	Works as part of a team	Jobs widely scattered	Initiative
	1	2	3	4	5	6	7	8	9	10	11	12	13	14	15	16	17	18	19	20	21	22	23
Optometrists				+	•	•	•					•	•	•	•	•	•	•	•		•	•	•
Osteopathic physicians				+	•	•	•		•		•		•	•	•	•	•	•	•		•	•	•
Physicians				+	•	•	•		•		•		•	•	•	•	•	•	•		•	•	•
Podiatrists				+	•	•	•					•	•	•	•	•	•	•	•		•	•	•
Veterinarians				+	•	•	•		•	•			•	•	•		•	•	•		•	•	•
Medical technologist, technician, and assistant occupations																							
Electrocardiograph technicians	•	T			•	•	•						•	•	•						•	•	
Electroencephalographic technologists and technicians	•	T			•	•	•						•	•	•						•	•	
Emergency medical technicians	•	T			•	•	•		•	•	•		•	•	•						•	•	
Medical laboratory workers	•	(²)	(²)	(²)	•		•	•				•	•	•							•	•	
Medical record technicians and clerks	•	(²)	(²)					•					•	•	•						•	•	
Operating room technicians		(³)	(³)		•	•	•	•					•	•	•						•	•	
Optometric assistants	•					•	•						•	•	•						•	•	
Radiologic (X-ray) technologists	•	•			•	•	•		•				•	•	•	•					•	•	
Respiratory therapy workers	•	(²)	(²)	(²)	•	•							•	•	•						•	•	
Nursing occupations																							
Registered nurses		(⁴)	(⁴)	(⁴)	•		•		•		•		•	•	•	•	•		•		•	•	•
Licensed practical nurses		T			•		•	•	•		•		•	•	•	•	•				•	•	
Nursing aides, orderlies, and attendants					•	•	•	•	•		•			•	•						•	•	
Therapy and rehabilitation occupations																							
Occupational therapists				•	•	•	•							•	•		•	•	•	•	•	•	•
Occupational therapy assistants		(²)	(²)			•	•							•	•	•	•	•			•	•	•
Physical therapists				•	•	•	•				•			•	•		•	•	•		•	•	•
Physical therapist assistants and aides		(²)	(²)		•	•					•			•	•		•				•	•	
Speech pathologists and audiologists				+	•	•	•						•	•	•	•	•	•	•		•	•	•
Other health occupations																							
Dietitians				•	•		•							•	•	•		•			•	•	•
Dispensing opticians	•	A			•	•							•	•	•						•	•	
Health services administrators				+	•									•			•	•	•		•	•	•
Medical record administrators				•	•								•	•				•			•	•	
Pharmacists				+	•		•					•	•	•	•						•	•	
SOCIAL SCIENTISTS																							
Anthropologists				+	•		(⁵)							•	(⁵)		•				•	•	
Economists				•	•		(⁵)							•	(⁵)		•				•	•	
Geographers				•	•	•	(⁵)							•	(⁵)		•				•	•	
Historians				+	•		(⁵)								•	(⁵)		•				•	•	
Political scientists				+	•		(⁵)							•	•		•				•	•	
Psychologists				+	•		•							•	•		•				•	•	
Sociologists				+	•		(⁵)							•	•		•				•	•	

1. Educational requirements vary by industry or employer.
2. Educational requirements vary according to type of work. See *Occupational Outlook Handbook* for details.

APPENDIX II

	High school	Tech. sch/Apprenticeship trng.	Junior college	College	Problem-solving ability	Uses tools, machinery	Instructs others	Repetitious work	Hazardous	Outdoors	Physical stamina	Generally confined	Precision	Works with detail	Frequent public contact	Part-time	Able to see results	Creativity	Influences others	Competition on the job	Works as part of a team	Jobs widely scattered	Initiative
	1	2	3	4	5	6	7	8	9	10	11	12	13	14	15	16	17	18	19	20	21	22	23
SOCIAL SERVICE OCCUPATIONS																							
Counseling occupations																							
School counselors				+	•		•							•	•		•	•		•		•	•
Employment counselors				+	•		•					•		•	•		•	•		•		•	•
Rehabilitation counselors				+	•		•							•	•		•	•		•		•	•
College career planning and placement counselors				+	•		•							•	•		•	•		•		•	•
Clergy																							
Protestant ministers				+	•		•								•			•	•		•	•	•
Rabbis				+	•		•								•			•	•		•	•	•
Roman Catholic priests				+	•		•								•			•	•		•	•	•
Other social service occupations																							
Cooperative extension service workers			•	•	•		•								•		•	•	•		•	•	•
Home economists			•	•	•		•								•		•	•	•		•	•	•
Homemaker-home health aides					•										•			•			•	•	
Park, recreation, and leisure service workers	•	(²)	(²)	(²)	•		•		•	•					•		•	•			•	•	•
Social service aides			•	•		•	•	•							•	•		•			•	•	
Social workers			•	•	•		•								•		•	•	•		•	•	•
ART, DESIGN, AND COMMUNICATIONS-RELATED OCCUPATIONS																							
Performing artists																							
Actors and actresses		T					(⁵)				•				•	•	•	•		•	•	•	
Dancers		T					(⁵)				•				•			•		•	•	•	
Musicians		T					(⁵)				•	•			•		•	•		•	•	•	
Singers		T					(⁵)				•				•		•	•		•	•	•	
Design occupations																							
Architects				•	•	•	•							•	•		•	•		•	•	•	•
Commercial artists	•	T				•								•			•	•		•	•	•	•
Display workers	•					•											•	•	•			•	•
Floral designers													•		•		•	•				•	
Industrial designers			•	•										•			•	•		•	•		•
Interior designers			•											•	•		•	•		•	•		•
Landscape architects			•	•										•	•		•	•		•	•		•
Photographers		(³)	(³)												•		•	•		•	•		•
Communications-related occupations																							
Interpreters			•												•	•							•
Newspaper reporters			•		•									•	•		•	•	•	•	•	•	•
Radio and television announcers			•				•							•	•		•	•	•	•	•	•	•
Technical writers			•	•										•			•	•		•	•	•	•

3 Training programs are available from vocational schools or junior colleges.
4. Diploma, baccalaureate, and associate degree programs prepare R.N. candidates for licensure. The baccalaureate degree is preferred for entry positions such as public health nurse, however, and is needed for advancement to supervisory positions or for clinical specialization.
5. Teachers only.

APPENDIX III.
GUIDE TO FEDERAL CAREER LITERATURE

CIVIL SERVICE COMMISSION PUBLICATIONS

(U.S. Civil Service Commission competitive examination *Announcements* can be obtained by writing to the nearest Federal Job Information Center.)

U.S. (BRE-67, also available in Spanish—BRE-68), write to: nearest Federal Job Information Center
  General information on the Federal employment process.

Working for the USA (BRE-37, also available in Spanish—BRE-44), write to: same as above
  All college majors. A more specific information booklet than *U.S.*, telling how to apply for a civil service job and what the Federal Government can offer you as a career employee.

Federal Jobs Overseas (BRE-18), write to: same as above
  Explains how overseas jobs are filled, discusses conditions of employment, indicates the kinds of skills agencies use, and lists addresses to which inquiries may be sent.

Beyond the BA (BRE-65, revised annually), write to: same as above

APPENDIX III

All college majors. A brief forecast of career opportunities for advanced degree graduates.

Trends in Federal Hiring, bi-annual. Copies available from the nearest Federal Job Information Center.
A newsletter for college and university placement directors and staff to provide timely, accurate, meaningful information about entry-level staffing needs in Federal agencies and the competitive situation in terms of hiring demand in relation to the supply of qualified candidates.

Federal Career Directory—A Guide for College Students (BRE-39), distributed to college placement offices nationwide. Individual copies can be obtained through the Government Printing Office.
All college majors. Comprehensive overview of Federal employment with emphasis on the major career occupations for college graduates. Includes nature of work, number of persons in the field, typical number of vacancies filled annually, and qualification requirements. Also contains information on each Federal agency, its principal missions and career fields.

Opportunities in the Federal Service for Veterans (BRE-48, revised annually), write to: same as above
Information on use of veterans preference in the Federal employment process.

DEPARTMENT PUBLICATIONS

Department of Agriculture

A Career for You in Agricultural Statistics, write to: Personnel Division, Economic Management Support Center, U.S. Department of Agriculture, 14th and Independence Avenue, S.W., Washington, DC 20250

ALTERNATIVE CAREERS FOR TEACHERS

College majors in agriculture, statistics, mathematics. Positions located nationwide. Outlines program activities of the Statistical Reporting Service and provides guidelines to the career opportunities available for those who meet requirements. Information on how to apply and location of positions are also included.

This is ERS, write to: same as above
Majors in economics. Positions located nationwide; some overseas opportunities. Describes the programs of the Economic Research Service and the opportunities offered the individual for specialization in research areas at the nationwide or regional level.

Scientific Careers in—(Variety of Titles), write to: Personnel Division, Agricultural Research Service, U.S. Department of Agriculture, Federal Building, Hyattsville, MD 20782
Primarily majors in agricultural, biological, and physical science. Positions located nationwide. A series of short leaflets covering employment opportunities and qualification requirements for positions with ARS.

Extension Home Economics, write to: Extension Service, U.S. Department of Agriculture, 14th and Independence Avenue, S.W., Washington, DC 20250
Majors in home economics. Positions located throughout the United States, Puerto Rico, Virgin Islands. Brief explanation of the Extension Home Economics Programs and what a Home Economist does. Includes family stability, consumer competence, housing and home furnishings, family health and community development.

Your Career as an Extension Agent, write to: same as above
Majors in agriculture, home economics, sociology, economics, or closely related fields. Positions located in United States, Puerto Rico, Virgin Islands, Guam. Describes a career as an extension agent including what the agent does, opportunities for advancement, and type of training given.

Forest Service Career Guide, write to: Personnel Management, P.O. Box 2417, U.S. Department of Agriculture, Washington, DC 20013

APPENDIX III

Majors in forestry, landscape architecture, geology, range conservation, soil science, hydrology, wildlife management, and engineering. Positions located nationwide. Describes career opportunities with the Forest Service. Includes qualification requirements and application procedures.

Careers in Soil Conservation Service, write to: same as above
Majors in soil conservation, engineering, soils, agricultural economics, forestry, range conservation, agronomy, wildlife biology, geology, related sciences. Positions located throughout the United States and Puerto Rico. Brief description of job opportunities as a soil conservationist, range conservationist, soil scientist, and engineer.

Department of Commerce

Career Gateways, write to: Employment Information Center, Room 1050L, Department of Commerce, 14th and Constitution Avenue, N.W., Washington, DC 20230
All college majors. Positions located worldwide. A thumbnail sketch of the Department of Commerce, general information about eligibility requirements, major career fields, and job locations.

Commodity Futures Trading Commission

For information about careers with CFTC, write: Office of Personnel, 2033 K Street, N.W., Washington, DC 20581
Majority of positions filled are futures trading specialists (investigators), economists, accountants, and attorneys. Desirable majors include business administration, finance, marketing, commerce, accounting, economics (especially agricultural economics), and law (JD or LLB degree). Positions located primarily in Washington, DC, New York, and Chicago.

ALTERNATIVE CAREERS FOR TEACHERS

Department of Defense

An Introduction to the Defense Logistics Agency, write to: Defense Logistics Agency (DLA), Chief, Staffing and Employee Relations Division, Cameron Station, Alexandria, VA 22314
  Describes the principal functions of the Agency. All college majors. Selections made primarily from the CSC Professional and Administrative Career Examination (PACE) Register, DLA Cooperative Education Program participants, and CSC Accounting Auditor Examination Register. Positions located nationwide.

Environmental Protection Agency

For information about careers with EPA, write to: Environmental Protection Agency, Washington, DC 20460, Attn: National Employment Center (PM–212)
  Majors in environmental engineering, sanitary engineering, mechanical engineering, chemical engineering, biology, toxicology, ecology, chemistry, environmental sciences, bioacoustics, pharmacology, and operations research.

Farm Credit Administration

Careers in Farm Credit Administration, write to: Personnel Division, Farm Credit Administration, Washington, DC 20578
  General description of the mission of Farm Credit Administration along with detailed information on career opportunities available to those with various academic backgrounds. Preferred majors include: business administration, economics, law, banking, finance, accounting, agricultural economics or agriculture. Most entry-level positions require professional accounting qualifications or master's degree or equivalent in agricultural economics.

APPENDIX III

Federal Communications Commission

The Federal Communications Commission and You, write to: Federal Communications Commission, Personnel Division, 1919 M Street, N.W., Room 208, Washington, DC 20554

    Majors in electrical engineering, law, accounting, liberal arts, electronics. Positions located nationwide. Describes FCC background and mission, career opportunities, advancement, and training.

Federal Maritime Commission

The Federal Maritime Commission and How it Functions, write to: Office of Personnel, Federal Maritime Commission, 1100 L Street, N.W., Washington, DC 20573

    Majors in law, transportation, business administration, accounting, or economics. A general description of the mission and organization of the Federal Maritime Commission.

Federal Power Commission

Careers in Meeting the Energy Crisis, write to: Director, Office of Personnel Programs, Federal Power Commission, 825 North Capitol Street, N.E., Washington, DC 20426

    Majors in petroleum, electrical and civil engineering, geology, economics, law, accounting-auditing, environment, fishery biology, outdoor recreation planning.

General Accounting Office

Work With GAO for More Effective Government, write to: Office of Personnel Development and Services, Room 7536, U.S.

General Accounting Office, 441 G Street, N.W., Washington, DC 20548
Majors in accounting, business economics, engineering, finance, management, mathematics, statistics and public administration. Positions located nationwide. Describes professional environment of GAO, the variety of assignments, and opportunities for professional development.

General Services Administration

Do it in 3, write to: College Relations Program Manager (BPE), General Services Administration, Washington, DC 20405
All college majors. Positions located nationwide. Outlines the mission and organization of the General Services Administration, the wide range of career opportunities and training programs available, and provides information on the location of GSA personnel offices and procedures for applying.

U.S. Government Printing Office

Opportunities at the United States Government Printing Office for College Graduates, write to: Chief, Employment Branch, Room C106, U.S. Government Printing Office, North Capitol and H Streets, N.W., Washington, DC 20401
Majors in printing management, library science, computer science, engineering, business administration, accounting, and liberal arts. Positions located in Washington, D.C. Printing Specialist positions also located nationwide. Contains general information about career opportunities with the U.S. Government Printing Office in such fields as printing management, general administration, procurement and supply, data processing, accounting, and library science.

APPENDIX III

Department of Health and Human Services

Career Opportunities at the National Institute of Health, write to: College Relations Officer, National Institutes of Health, Bethesda, MD 20014

All college majors. Positions located in Bethesda, MD. Describes NIH Management Intern program as well as opportunities in administrative and technical fields.

Career Opportunities for the College Graduate, write to: College Relations Officer, Social Security Administration, Baltimore, MD 21235

All college majors. Positions located nationwide. Outlines opportunities for college graduates in Social Security Administration.

Consumer Safety Officer, A career with FDA, write to: DHEW, PHS, Division of Personnel Management, FDA, 5600 Fishers Lane, Rockville, MD 20857

Majors in science. Positions located nationwide. Describes work of FDA consumer safety officers.

Department of Housing and Urban Development

Careers with HUD, write to: Director of Recruitment, Department of HUD, Washington, DC 20410

Describes the Department's functions and organization, briefly outlines major recruitment needs and how to apply.

Interstate Commerce Commission

Career Opportunities, write to: Director of Personnel, Interstate Commerce Commission, Washington, DC 20423

All majors. Positions nationwide. Describes career fields of ICC and structure of the agency.

Become a Transportation Specialist, write to: same as above
Majors in business administration, economics, transportation. Positions located nationwide. Description of ICC and work of transportation specialists.

Department of Interior

Career Opportunities—Bureau of Reclamation, write to: Bureau of Reclamation, Department of the Interior, Washington, DC 20240
Majors in civil, electrical, hydraulic, mechanical and agricultural engineering, meteorology, economics, geology, agronomy, accounting, environmental management, outdoor recreation, computer science, archeology, and journalism. Describes the various professional and technical career occupations utilized nationwide within the Bureau of Reclamation.

Working for the Bureau of Outdoor Recreation, write to: Bureau of Outdoor Recreation, Department of the Interior, Washington, DC 20240
Majors in Biological Science, Natural Resource Management and Conservation, social science, design and planning, or earth science, sociology, forestry, economics, geography, urban or regional planning, and outdoor recreation. Positions located nationwide. Describes Bureau's mission and nature of work.

Opportunities in Resource Management, write to: Bureau of Land Management, Department of the Interior, Washington, DC 20240
Majors in forestry, engineering, biology, geology, mineral economy, oceanography, ecology, wildlife biology. Positions located nationwide. General introduction to career opportunities in Resource Management. Describes Bureau programs and positions available.

Career Outlines—National Park Service, write to: National Park Service, Department of the Interior, Washington, DC 20240

APPENDIX III

Majors in sciences, engineering, history, archeology, architecture, landscape architecture, resource management, park and recreation management, police science. Positions located nationwide. Describes the work and job opportunities with the National Park Service. Designed to answer the most frequently asked questions from individuals seeking career information.

Department of Justice

FBI Career Opportunities, write to: Personnel Officer, FBI, J. Edgar Hoover Building, Washington, DC 20535
   Briefly describes many career opportunities within the FBI as well as benefits available to employees.

Department of Labor

Major Professional Occupations, write to: Office of Special Personnel Services, New Department of Labor Building, 200 Constitution Avenue, N.W., Washington, DC 20210
   Majors in economics, statistics, business administration, computer science, political science, accounting, public administration, industrial relations, social sciences, chemistry, and engineering. Positions are located nationwide. General information is provided on the qualifications for major professional careers in the Department.

National Credit Union Administration

The National Credit Union Administration, write to: Director of Personnel, National Credit Union Administration, Washington, DC 20456

Majors in business administration. Describes the National Credit Union Administration, the job of examiner, and the qualifications required.

National Labor Relations Board

A Career in Labor-Management Relations as a Field Examiner, write to: Director of Personnel, Room 300, National Labor Relations Board, 1717 Pennsylvania Avenue, N.W., Washington, DC 20570
   Majors in labor relations, industrial relations, personnel administration, business administration, economics, labor economics, labor law, political science, accounting, law. Positions located nationwide. Describes career opportunities in the National Labor Relations Board for college graduates.

National Security Agency

Professional Qualifications Test Bulletin, National Security Agency, write to: Chief, College Recruitment Program, National Security Agency, Fort George G. Meade, MD 20755, Attn: M321
   Majors in mathematics and language. Describes qualifications, test and application procedures, opportunities, and career fields.

Careers for Engineers, Mathematicians, and Computer Scientists at the National Security Agency, write to: same as above
   Majors in mathematics, computer science, engineering, and physics. Describes career opportunities and benefits.

National Security Agency/Central Security Service, write to: same as above
   Majors in electronic engineering, physics, mathematics, linguistics, and computer science. Describes opportunities and challenges in the fields of cryptography, computer science, and the research and development of communications equipment.

NSA Technical Journals, Special Linguistics Issue, Special Mathematics and Engineering Issue, and Special Computer and Information Sciences Issue, write to: same as above
> Majors in linguistics, mathematics, engineering and computer science.

Securities and Exchange Commission

Securities and Exchange Commission: A Sound Investment in Your Future as a Financial Analyst, write to: Director of Personnel, Securities and Exchange Commission, 500 North Capitol Street, Washington, DC 20549
> Majors in business administration, finance, accounting, economics. Positions located in Washington, DC. Describes responsibilities of SEC, location of positions, duties, salaries, benefits, career opportunities, and recruitment policy.

Department of State

Examination for Foreign Service Officer Careers, revised annually, write to: Board of Examiners for the Foreign Service, Department of State, Washington, DC 20520
> All majors. Positions located worldwide. Describes the Foreign Service Officer Corps and the examination process, including requirements and sample questions, and contains application for examination.

Department of Treasury

IRS . . . Let Us Fit Into Your Future, write to: College Recruitment Coordinator at the nearest Internal Revenue Service district office. This package of material contains general information about the IRS and specified information about various occupations. When writing, specify the area or occupation in which you are interested.

Tax Auditor. All college majors, courses of study in business-related subjects recommended. Positions located nationwide. The Tax Auditor is a specialist in resolving Federal income tax questions on individual and small business returns.

Revenue Officer. All college majors; courses of study in business-related subjects recommended. Positions located nationwide. The Revenue Officer is a field worker with the responsibility of collecting unpaid taxes and helping people understand and meet their tax obligations.

Internal Security Inspector. Any major. Positions nationwide. Conducts a variety of investigations related to internal IRS operations. Applicants must not have reached 35th birthday at time of appointment.

U.S. Customs Service

Exceptional Careers, (nine leaflets in folder), write to: Regional Personnel Officer in the nearest Customs Regional Personnel Office or the Headquarters Personnel Branch in Washington, DC

This packet provides general information on the Customs Service, specific information on major Customs occupations, qualification requirements, duties, career advancement opportunities, benefits, etc. Positions are located nationwide and most college majors are acceptable; courses of study in business and law enforcement are recommended.

Bureau of Alcohol, Tobacco, and Firearms

The Bureau has available two brief pamphlets describing the qualifications and duties for Special Agents and Inspectors. These pamphlets can be obtained from their regional personnel offices in New York City, Philadelphia, Atlanta, Chicago, Cincinnati, Dallas, and San Francisco or by writing to: Bureau of Alcohol, Tobacco and Firearms, Employment Branch, Room 2226, 1200 Pennsylvania Avenue, N.W., Washington, DC 20226. Please specify the occupation of interest.

United States Information Agency

Global Communications Revolution, write to: Special Programs, USIA–IPT, Room 508, 1717 Pennsylvania Avenue, Washington, DC 20597
> No special college major required, but liberal arts, arts, political science, journalism, broadcasting, and languages are useful. Most positions located in Washington, DC. Names and explains the kinds of Civil Service jobs (as distinguished from Foreign Service jobs, which are separate and distinct at USIA) available in the agency.

Veterans Administration

For any of the following VA pamphlets, order by citing the pamphlet number and writing to: VA Forms and Publications Depot, 2625 Shirlington Road, Arlington, VA 22206.

Librarians in Veterans Administration Hospitals (VA Pamphlet 10–61)
> Majors in library science. Positions located nationwide, primarily for MSL's. Includes information about work assignments, VA's paid work-study program for graduate students, work locations, and qualifications required.

The Social Worker—in the VA (VA Pamphlet IB 10–16)
> Majors in social work (with master's degree). Describes employment opportunities for clinical social workers in VA Hospitals and Clinics nationwide. Includes information about casework, supervision, research, and administration in medical and psychiatric social work.

ALTERNATIVE CAREERS FOR TEACHERS

Therapists, Rehabilitation—in the Veterans Administration (VA Pamphlet IB 10-7)
   Majors in correctional, occupational, or physical therapy, industrial arts, recreation, or physical education. Positions located in VA Hospitals nationwide. Contains information about duties in various areas of therapy, administration, education, and research.

Administrative Careers in the Veterans Administration (VA Pamphlet 05-50)
   All college majors. Positions located nationwide. Describes duties and training opportunities for various administrative specialties in fields such as supply, personnel, management analysis, building management, medical administration, fiscal management, loan guaranty, veterans benefits counseling, claims examining, and cemetery administration. Most of these positions require eligibility in the Professional and Administrative Career Examination.

Data Processing in the Veterans Administration (VA Pamphlet 30-1)
   All college majors. Positions located nationwide. Describes employment opportunities, including traineeships for programmers, systems analysts, computer operators, and computer technicians.

Careers for Voluntary Service Officers (VA Pamphlet IB 10-4)
   For majors in recreation, public relations, physical education, education, psychology, social work, or hospital administration. Positions located in VA Hospitals nationwide. Describes employment opportunities, including traineeships, and includes information on the Volunteer program in the Veterans Administration.

BIBLIOGRAPHY

Bestor, Dorothy K. *Aside from Teaching, What in the World Can You Do?: Career Strategies for Liberal Arts Graduates*. Seattle, Washington: University of Washington Press, 1982.

Bolles, Richard N. *The Three Boxes of Life*. Berkeley, California: Ten Speed Press, 1978.

———. *What Color is Your Parachute? A Practical Manual for Job Hunters and Career Changers*. Berkeley, California: Ten Speed Press, 1984.

Campbell, David. *If You Don't Know Where You're Going, You'll Probably End Up Someplace Else*. Niles, Illinois: Argus Communications, 1974.

Catalyst. *Resume Preparation Manual: A Step-by-Step Guide for Women*. New York: Catalyst, 1976.

Catalyst Staff. *Marketing Yourself*. New York: G.P. Putnam's Sons, 1980.

Cox, Keith and Ben M. Enis, Eds. *A New Measure of Responsibility for Marketing*. Chicago, Illinois: American Marketing Association, 1968.

Cudney, Milton R. *Eliminating Self-Defeating Behavior*. Kalamazoo, Michigan: Life Giving Enterprises, 1975.

Djeddah, Eli. *Moving Up*. Berkeley, California: Ten Speed Press, 1983.

Dictionary of Occupational Titles. U.S. Department of Labor. Washington, D.C.: Government Printing Office, 5th Ed.

Encyclopedia of Associations, National Organizations of the United States. Detroit, Michigan: Gale Research Company, 1984.

Figler, Howard E. *The Complete Job Search Handbook: All the Skills You Need to Get Any Job and Have a Good Time Doing It*. New York, New York: Holt, Rinehart and Winston, 1979.

Gates, Anita. *90 Most Promising Careers for the 80's*. New York: Simon and Schuster, 1982.

Ginn, Robert J. Jr. *The College Graduate's Career Guide*. New York: Charles Scribner's Sons, 1981.

Hillstrom, J. K. *Steps to Professional Employment with Special Advice for Liberal Arts Graduates*. Woodbury, New York: Barron's Educational Services, Inc. 1982.

Hopke, William E. Ed. *Encyclopedia of Career and Vocational Guidance*. Volumes I and II. Chicago, Illinois: Ferguson Publishing, 1982.

Hoppock, Robert. *Occupational Information: Where to Get It and How to Use It in Counseling and in Teaching*. 3rd Ed. New York: McGraw Hill, 1967.

Irish, Richard K. *Go Hire Yourself an Employer*. Revised and expanded edition. Garden City, New York: Anchor Press, 1978.

Kennedy, Marilyn Moats. *Salary Strategies: Everything You Need to Know to Get the Salary You Want*. New York, New York: Rawson, Wade Publishers, 1982.

Lewis, Adele. *How to Write Better Resumes*. Woodbury, New York: Barron's Educational Services, Inc., 1977.

Lichty, Jacqueline. *The Educator's Job Change Manual*. Troy, Michigan: Phoenix Services, 1981.

BIBLIOGRAPHY

Medley, H. Anthony. *Sweaty Palms, The Neglected Art of Being Interviewed*. Belmont, California: Lifetime Learning Publications, 1978.

Merman, Stephen K. and John E. McLaughlin. *Out-Interviewing the Interviewer: A Job Winner's Script for Success*. Englewood Cliffs, New Jersey: Prentice-Hall, Inc., 1983.

Moving to..... Annual. Winchester, Virginia: James Publishing Co., 1981.

Munschauer, John L. *Jobs for English Majors and Other Smart People*. Princeton, New Jersey: Peterson's Guides, 1982.

Occupational Outlook Handbook. 1984–1985 Ed. U.S. Department of Labor: Bureau of Labor Statistics, Washington, D.C. Government Printing Office.

Orstein, Allan C. "Teacher Salaries: Past, Present, Future." *Phi Delta Kappan*, 61 (June, 1980), 677-79.

Peale, Norman Vincent. *The Positive Principle Today*. Carmel, New York: Guideposts, 1976.

Resume Service Staff. *Resumes That Get Jobs*. New York, New York: ARCO Publishing, Inc., 1981.

Rockcastle, Madeline T. Ed/Author. *"Where to Start." An Annotated Career Planning Bibliography*. 1983–85 4th Edition. Princeton, New Jersey: Peterson's Guides.

Stark, Joan S. "From the Dean: Keeping Score." *Innovator*, Vol. 12, No. 10 (July 27, 1981), 2–3.

———. "From the Dean: News from the Front Lines." *Innovator*, Vol. 13, No. 1 (Sept. 21, 1981), 2–4.

———. "From the Dean: Strayed Sheep." *Innovator*, Vol. 12, No. 8 (March 30, 1981), 2–3.

Stark, Joan S., A.E. Austin, M.A. Lowther, D.W. Chapman, and S.M. Hutcheson. *Teacher Certification Recipients at The University of Michigan 1946 through 1976: A 1980 Follow-up Study*. Ann Arbor, Michigan: The University of Michigan.

Wright, John W. *The American Almanac of Jobs and Salaries*. New York, New York: Avon Books, 1982.

AUTHORS' NOTE

WE WOULD LIKE TO HEAR FROM YOU. The revisions for this second printing were made on the basis of the valuable input we received from educators who read the first edition. We welcome your comments. You can mail your suggestions to us at this address:

    Marna L. Beard and/or Michael J. McGahey
    24917 Star Valley
    St. Clair Shores
    Michigan 48080

INDEX

Abilities, checklist of, 40–43
Agricultural education major, 60–62
Anxiety, 11, 13
Art major, 63–66
Assertiveness, 50
Associations, professional, 174
Autonomy
    achieved through skill proficiency, 39
    teachers' skill in, 7
    valued in new careers, 9, 19, 20, 27

Biology major, 66–69
Blockages, career change, 144, 183–190
Bolles, Richard N., 35, 177
Bulletins, college placement, 176
Business education major, 69–72

Career alternative descriptions, 58–136
    acquisitions librarian, 109
    actuary, 111
    admissions evaluator/counselor, 129
    agricultural commodities inspector, 61, 67
    agricultural county agent, 60
    agriculture market research analyst, 62
    airplane-flight attendant, 88
    appraiser, 78
    archivist, 98, 110
    art conservator, 64
    assistant buyer, 102
    assistant curator, 97
    assistant director, music, 115
    bank officer, 79
    bibliographer, 109
    biographer, 97
    biologist, 68
    book critic, 110
    booking manager, 116
    bookkeeper, 132
    budget officer, 77
    business owner, school supplies, 24
    camp director, 117
    cartographic technician, 91
    caseworker, child welfare, 135
    caseworker, social service, 129

chemical-laboratory technician, 75
claims adjustor, 61
claims examiner, 71
college career planning and placement counselor, 128
colorist, 74
columnist/commentator, 105
community relations worker, 126
computer operator, 25
construction inspector, 103
cooperative extension service worker, 101
copywriter, 107
counselor
    admissions evaluator, 129
    career planning and placement, 128
    vocational advisor, 130
county agricultural agent, 60
credit analyst, 78
credit manager, 70, 125
customs import specialist, 95
dental ceramist, 65
department store assistant buyer, 64
dictionary editor, 85
director
    camp, 117
    fundraising, 115
    historical society, 98
    hospital recreation, 117
    music, assistant, 115
    social, 118
drafter, 104
educational technician, health, 14
educational training instructor, 83
educational consultant, 18
educational representative for a newspaper, 19
employment interviewer, 85
encyclopedia research worker, 85
environmental analyst, 67
financial analyst, 79, 113
financial report service, sales agent, 71
food and drug inspector, 75, 121
food products tester, 101
food technologist, 68
foreign banknote teller-trader, 87

INDEX

foreign correspondent, 88
foreign exchange code clerk, 88
foreign service officer, 123
foreign student advisor, 88
foreign trade services clerk, 88
foreign translator/stenographer, 87
Four-H club agent, 100
franchise sales agent, 86
health education technician, 14
home service representative, 100
hospital recreation director, 117
illustrator, 63
    technical, 65, 104
immigration inspector, 93
import-export agent, 123
importer/exporter, 86, 89
information scientist, 110
inspector, industrial waste, 67, 95
instructor,
    correspondence school, 132
    private business school, 71
instrument repairer, music, 115
insurance sales agent, 98
insurance underwriter, 70, 113
intelligence specialist, 124
interior designer, 63, 100
interpreter, 87
interviewer, 135
    employment, 85
    loan, 82
lease buyer, mining, 95
librarian,
    acquisition, 109
    special, 109
loan counselor, 112
loan interviewer, 82
loan officer, 77
lobbyist, 124
malt-specification control assistant, 75
manager
    booking, 22, 116
    concert, 116
    credit, 70, 125
    display, 71
    hotel recreation facility, 118
    merchandise, 101
    nursery school, 82
    office, 132
    personnel, 81
map editor, 92
market research analyst, 23, 73
    agricultural, 62
merchandise displayer, 63
merchandise manager, 101
music
    assistant director, 115

    teacher, private, 115
musical instrument repairer, 115
newswriter, 107
nursery school manager, 82
office manager, 132
operations research analyst, 112
outreach coordinator for historical society, 17
parole officer, 130
patent examiner, 121
patternmaker, 102
personnel
    coordinator of QWL program, 21
    psychologist, 125
    recruiter, 127
petroleum laboratory assistant, 94
photojournalist, 65
physicist, 121
pollster, 124, 134
private music teacher, 115
probation officer, 126
psychological tests and industrial relations sales agent, 126
public relations representative, 106
publishers' representative, 109
quality control technician, 74, 120
real estate sales agent, 100
recreational supervisor, 82
recreational leader, 117
register representative, 13
reporter, 79, 84
research analyst, 93
    agriculture market, 62
    market, general, 73
    operations, 112
research assistant, 97
sales agent
    franchise, 86
    financial report services, 71
    insurance, 98
    psychological tests and industrial relations, 126
    real estate, 100
    securities, 77
sales representative, 16, 27
    chemicals and drugs, 67
    computers and EDP systems, 112
    dental and medical equipment and supplies, 120
    educational courses, 104
    farm and garden equipment and supplies, 61
    hobbies and crafts, 64
    manufacturer's clothes, 101
    musical instruments and accessories, 115
    office machines, 70

oilfield supplies and equipment, 95
petroleum products, 96
pharmaceutical products, 73
playground equipment, 82
poultry, equipment and supplies, 60
publications, 85
recreation and sporting goods, 117
school equipment and supplies, 81
sheet music, 116
traffic agent, 92
welding equipment, 104
school programs supervisor, utility company, 26
science editor, 121
securities sales agent, 77
social director, 118
soil conservationist, 61
special librarian, 109
sports announcer, 118
state police officer, 134
statistician, 112
stockbroker, 20
technical illustrator, 65, 104
technical writer, 106
tester, food products, 101
textile designer, 64
training representative, 15, 83
translator, 89
travel agent, 87, 98
underwriter, insurance, 70, 113
urban planning aide, 92
vocational counselor/advisor, 130
water purification chemist, 74
writer, free-lance, 18
writer, technical, 84, 106
yeast culture developer, 75
Career change
 adjustments, 8–10
 blockages, 144, 183–190
 experience of others, 13–28
 financial considerations, 31–34
 process, defined, 11, 182–198
 routes, possible, 18
 steps and stages, 30
 support groups, 16
 timing considerations, 30–31
Career development
 educators' leadership in, 21
 personal, 5
Career environment options, 51–55
 areas of work, 51–52
 relating to others, 53
 settings, 53–54
 work activities, 52
 values, 54–55
Career options
 by certification area, 58–136

by personal and job characteristics, 219–229
frequently chosen, 4
within the federal government, 59, 199–218
see also: career alternative descriptions
Career options, form for recording, 140
Career planning, a model, 183
Career research
 incomes, 33
 occupational information resources, 137–139, 142–143
Certification
 career options by teaching area of, 58–136
 dependence on, 7
Chemistry major, 73–76
Chronological resume, 151–152, 161
College Graduate, The Occupational Outlook for, 138
College Placement Annual, The, 138
Commitment to action, 11–12
Cover letter, 168–170
Creating a career, 17–18
Credentials, dependence on, 7

Dictionary of Occupational Titles, 1–2
Dun and Bradstreet report, 178

Economics major, 76–80
Elementary education major, 81–83
Employer's view of teachers, 16, 26
Employment agencies, 175–176
 as screening agents, 175
 private, 175–176
 public, 175
 utilization of, 176
Encyclopedia of Career and Vocational Guidance, 138
English major, 83–86

Foreign language major, 86–90
Fringe benefits, 34
Functional resumes, 151–152
 Samples of, 162–167
 Tips for preparing, 159–160

Geographic directories, 178
Geography major, 91–94
Geology major, 94–96

Hidden job market, 150
History major, 96–99
Home Economics major, 99–103

INDEX

Imagination/imagining, 10–11
Income
  loss, 25
  moonlighting to supplement, 33
  potential, 25
  teachers vs. non-educators, 3, 32
Individual assessment, 39–57, 191, 195–196
Industrial arts major, 103–105
Industry directories, 178
Informational interviews, 147–149, 150, 184
Interests
  analysis of, 51–55
  data-people-things, 45
  pursuing, 18
Interviewing, 178–180
  evaluation of, 180
  follow-up to, 180–181
  informational, 147–149, 150, 184
  research prior to, 178–179
  suggestions for, 179–180
Interviews, obtaining leads, 142–143, 173–178

Job, selecting your ideal, 56
Job characteristics and personal preferences, matching of, 219–229
Job leads, sources of, 173–178
  college placement offices, 176
  employment agencies, 175–176
  journals, 174–175
  networking, 15, 142–146, 174
  newspaper ads, 177
  placement bulletins, 176
  professional associations and publications, 174–175
Job objective, 157–158
Job research sheet, worksheet, 141
Job satisfactions, comparisons, 8
Job security, 18
Job titles
  definitions. *See* listing under career alternative descriptions
  variation of meaning, 58–59
Jobs, by college major, 58–136
Jobs within the federal government, 59, 199–218
Journalism major, 105–108
Journals, 174–175

Leaves of absence, 34
Liberal Arts graduates, 146
Library science major, 108–111
Literature, guide to federal career, 230–244

Marketing defined, 171
Marketing your skills
  approaches and strategies, 171–181, 194
  creative approach, 177–178
  mass mailing approach, 177
  philosophy of, 171
  preparation for, 171–173, 192–194
  sources of job leads for, 173–178
Mass mailing resumes, 177
Mathematics major, 111–114
McNair, Malcolm P., 171
Middle Market Directory, Dun and Bradstreet, 178
Million Dollar Directory, Dun and Bradstreet, 178
Model, career planning, 183
Music education major, 114–116

National Advertising Register, 178
Networking, 15, 142–146, 149, 151, 156
Newspaper ads, 177

Occupational descriptions, see career alternative descriptions
Occupational forecasts, 138
Occupational information, 137–139, 191–192
Occupational information systems, 139–140
Occupational Outlook Handbook, 137
Occupational Outlook for College Graduates, 138
Occupational Outlook Quarterly, 138
Occupations, frequent career alternatives, 4
Original research, 142

Personal and job characteristics, matching, 219–229
Personality strengths analysis, 46–50
Personnel work, variety in, 59
Physical education/recreation major, 116–119
Physics major, 119–122
Placement offices, college or university, 176
Platform skills, 153
Political science major, 122–125
Positive thinking, 11, 34–37, 188
Professional associations and publications, 174–175
Promotion, strategies for achieving, 5–8, 15, 18, 21–23
Psychology major, 125–127

253

Publications, professional, 174–175

Researching occupational information, 137–142
Researching specific companies or organizations, 178–179
Resumes, 150–170
  action words, 40–44, 154, 156
  cover letter, 168–169
  focus, 150, 154
  forms of, 151–152
  recordkeeping, 169–170
  samples of, 161–167
  screening by recipient, 17, 35, 150
  statements, 152–157
  writing tips, 45, 147, 159–160
Retraining, 7–8
Rewards of changing careers, 8–10

School counselor major, 128–131
Secretarial science major, 131–134
Self assessment, 39–57, 191, 195–196
Self-employment, 16, 19, 24, 27
Self-management skills, analysis of, 46–50
Skills, teachers'
  acquisition through teaching, 7
  analysis of, 18, 26–27
  checklist of, 40–43
  in communication, 6–7, 153
  in data analysis, 2
  in leadership, 7
  in learning, 1, 7, 14, 19, 23, 25
  in managing, 2, 6
  perception of, 1, 3, 27
  problem solving, 2
  public speaking, 3, 13, 153
  sales, 6, 27–28
  transference of, 5–8. *See* all of Chapter 2
  writing, 6, 19, 23
Sociology major, 134–136
Standard and Poors' *Dictionary of Directors*, 178
Stark, Joan S., 3, 32
Stock market reports, 178
Stress in teaching, 9–10

Teaching
  frequently chosen alternative to, 4
  majors and alternative careers, 58–136. *See* certification and career alternative descriptions
  preparation for other work, 19
  rephrasing the experience of, 27–28
  skills involved in, 1–7, 13–28
  typical tasks, 2
Thank you letter, 181
Thomas' Register of American Manufacturing, 178
Traditional resume, 151–152
Training programs, 13–14, 23

Value options, 54–55
Volunteer work, 19

Work setting options, 53–54